The Economics of Crime

R. W. ANDERSON

Formerly of the Institute of Social and Economic Research
University of York

M

First published 1976 by
THE MACMILLAN PRESS LTD
London and Basingstoke
Associated companies in New York Dublin
Melbourne Johannesburg and Madras

SBN 333 16899 2

Printed in Great Britain by
THE ANCHOR PRESS LTD
Tiptree, Essex

H3

Editors' Preface to Macmillan Studies in Economics

The rapid growth of academic literature in the field of economics has posed serious problems for both students and teachers of the subject. The latter find it difficult to keep pace with more than few areas of the subject so that an inevitable trend towards specialism emerges. The student quickly loses perspective as the maze of theories and models grows, particularly at a time when so much reappraisal of the established paradigms is taking place.

The aim of the 'Macmillan Studies in Economics' is to offer students, and perhaps some teachers as well, short, reasonably critical overviews of developments in selected areas of economics, particularly those in which current controversies are to be found. As far as possible the titles have been selected to form an integrated whole, although inevitably whole areas have been neglected as being unsuited to the style, format and length of the titles in the series.

In some cases the volumes are rather more like essays than surveys. In most cases, however, the aim is to survey the salient literature in a critical fashion. The level of understanding required to read the volumes varies with the complexity of the subject, but they have been generally written to suit the second- and third-year undergraduate seeking to place his reading of the detailed literature in an over-all context. They are *not* textbooks. Instead they seek to give the kind of perspective that might well be lost by reading longer textbooks on their own, or by reading articles in journals. In particular, they should be most suited to pre-examination revision periods. They are not intended to substitute for the essential reading and assimilation of the original works that they seek to survey and assess.

MACMILLAN STUDIES IN ECONOMICS

Published

R. W. Anderson: THE ECONOMICS OF CRIME
John Burton: WAGE INFLATION
Ben Fine: MARX'S 'CAPITAL'
Douglas Fisher: MONETARY POLICY
Miles Fleming: MONETARY THEORY
C. J. Hawkins and D. W. Pearce: CAPITAL INVESTMENT APPRAISAL
C. J. Hawkins: THEORY OF THE FIRM
David F. Heathfield: PRODUCTION FUNCTIONS
Dudley Jackson: POVERTY
P. N. Junankar: INVESTMENT: THEORIES AND EVIDENCE
J. E. King: LABOUR ECONOMICS
John King and Philip Regan: RELATIVE INCOME SHARES
J. A. Kregel: THE THEORY OF ECONOMIC GROWTH
J. A. Kregel: THEORY OF CAPITAL
Richard Lecomber: ECONOMIC GROWTH VERSUS THE ENVIRONMENT
George McKenzie: THE MONETARY THEORY OF INTERNATIONAL TRADE
David J. Mayston: THE IDEA OF SOCIAL CHOICE
C. A. Nash: PUBLIC VERSUS PRIVATE TRANSPORT
S. K. Nath: A PERSPECTIVE OF WELFARE ECONOMICS
Anthony Peaker: ECONOMIC GROWTH IN MODERN BRITAIN
D. W. Pearce: COST-BENEFIT ANALYSIS
Maurice Peston: PUBLIC GOODS AND THE PUBLIC SECTOR
Nicholas Rau: TRADE CYCLES: THEORY AND EVIDENCE
David Robertson: INTERNATIONAL TRADE POLICY
Charles K. Rowley: ANTITRUST AND ECONOMIC EFFICIENCY
C. H. Sharp: TRANSPORT ECONOMICS
G. K. Shaw: FISCAL POLICY
R. Shone: THE PURE THEORY OF INTERNATIONAL TRADE
M. J. Stabler: AGRICULTURAL ECONOMICS AND RURAL LAND-USE
Frank J. B. Stilwell: REGIONAL ECONOMIC POLICY
A. P. Thirlwall: FINANCING ECONOMIC DEVELOPMENT
John Vaizey: THE ECONOMICS OF EDUCATION
J. van Doorn: DISEQUILIBRIUM ECONOMICS
Peter A. Victor: ECONOMICS OF POLLUTION
Grahame Walshe: INTERNATIONAL MONETARY REFORM
Michael G. Webb: PRICING POLICIES FOR PUBLIC ENTERPRISES
E. Roy Weintraub: CONFLICT AND CO-OPERATION IN ECONOMICS
E. Roy Weintraub: GENERAL EQUILIBRIUM THEORY

Forthcoming

S. Charles: HOUSING ECONOMICS
C. Collier and K. Turner: ECONOMICS OF PLANNING
B. Morgan: MONETARISM AND KEYNESIANISM
A. Ziderman: MANPOWER TRAINING: THEORY AND POLICY

Contents

Acknowledgements

First, I should like to proclaim my indebtedness to Alan Williams who acted as accessory before the fact in encouraging me to write this book. Second, thanks are due to David Pearce for his patience and encouragement as the chapters rolled into him as editor and for his attempts to deflect me from the wilder excesses which I had perpetrated. Third, I should like to thank the participants in a Royal Economic Society conference on 'Resource Allocation in the Public Sector' for their comments on a paper I presented on cost–benefit analysis in the criminal justice system; special thanks are due to M. V. Posner, editor of the conference proceedings. None of the above shares responsibility for the errors, omissions and obscurities which may be detected. Finally, the book was written while the author was a member of the Public Sector Studies Group at the Institute of Social and Economic Research and the Department of Economics at the University of York; gratitude is due to the S.S.R.C. which finances the Group's research programme.

R.W.A.

Introduction

This book is concerned with the economics of crime prevention. It is doubtful whether the potential criminal will find in it much that is to his private advantage. In the parlance of historians, it is a secondary work the main objective of which is exposition of the literature. In one or two places, however, an attempt is made to extend the two basic models – those of Ehrlich [1] and Becker [2] – in certain rather obvious ways, notably in Chapters 5 and 6. A low ceiling has been placed on the level of mathematical sophistication expected of the reader: there is nothing beyond partial differentiation – not even Lagrangean multipliers.

It should be noted that, throughout, the conceptual framework of welfare economics is applied. The objective is to identify policies which will produce potential Pareto improvements. Individuals, even those who break laws, are assumed to be the best judges of their own welfare. In the absence of any statement to the contrary it should be assumed that all parties' costs and benefits are being counted and are being given the subjective valuations of the parties themselves so far as that is possible. Though laymen, criminologists, sociologists and others are fond of drawing a distinction between economic and non-economic crimes, this is not an easy task and one that we shall not attempt. On the contrary, it is useful to have money values for 'non-economic' crimes to ensure their commensurability with 'economic' crimes and the commensurability of both with the inputs of crime-prevention resources which can, on the whole, readily be expressed in money terms.

1 The Supply and Control of Offences

The purpose of this chapter is to identify the variables which society can manipulate in an effort to control the number of offences committed. First it is necessary to establish a theory of the supply of offences. Offending as an activity shares important features with other occupations in that an individual is committing his time, effort and resources – all of which have valuable alternative uses – in the hope of reaping a reward. The main elements affecting occupational choice are (i) the pecuniary and non-pecuniary rewards of the contemplated occupation, (ii) those of alternative occupations, and (iii) individual taste. We shall have little to say about tastes. In general these may be taken to be dealt with by the device of considering subjective values of rewards.

We shall find it most useful to proceed in the context of Ehrlich's fruitful model of the supply of offences [1]. A key feature of illicit activity is the uncertainty of its outcome: the rewards of offending and getting away with it are different to those of offending and being caught. The rewards of legitimate activity, on the other hand, are assumed to be certain. Though not of course strictly true, this assumption is a helpful simplification of a complex problem.

Ehrlich [1] further simplifies the choice situation by considering only one period of time during which one of only two states of the world can occur: (*a*) the offender is caught and punished, (*b*) he is not caught and therefore not punished. The model satisfies the conditions to which state-preference theory can be applied. A full exposition of state-preference theory is to be found in Green ([3] ch. 15).

Let X_a denote the money value of the offender's pecuniary and non-pecuniary costs and benefits if state (*a*) occurs – that is he is caught – and X_b if state (*b*) occurs. The offender is assumed to have a fixed time budget, t, to devote to legitimate and illegitimate activities, a fixed amount of time for consumption and leisure having been allowed for. If t_i is the time devoted to illegitimate activities, $t-t_i$ is the time devoted to legitimate activity, assuming for the moment that the individual does not opt wholly for one or the other. Then,

$$X_a = W + W_i(t_i) + W_l(t-t_i) - F_i(t_i)$$

and

$$X_b = W + W_i(t_i) + W_l(t-t_i),$$

where W_i and W_l are the returns from illegitimate and legitimate activity respectively and F_i is the money value of the punishment imposed if state (a) occurs. W is the value of such of the individual's wealth (broadly defined) as does not depend on the outcome of his labours. The following restrictions ensure diminishing marginal returns in both states:

$$W_i', W_l', F_i' > 0; \quad W_i'', W_l'' < 0, \quad F_i'' > 0.$$

The probability of capture and punishment is p, assumed not to depend on t_i; the probability of non-capture is therefore $1-p$.

The individual's expected utility is equal to the sum of the utilities of the two states weighted by their probabilities, that is

$$EU = pU(X_a) + (1-p)U(X_b),$$

where $U(X)$ is the utility-of-wealth function. Substituting for X_a and X_b,

$$EU = pU[W + W_i(t_i) + W_l(t-t_i) - F_i(t_i)] + (1-p)U[W + W_i(t_i) + W_l(t-t_i)].$$

The individual will adjust t_i to maximise expected utility, such that

$$\frac{dEU}{dt_i} = pU'(X_a)[W_i'(t_i) - W_l'(t-t_i) - F_i'(t_i)] + (1-p)U'(X_b)[W_i'(t_i) - W_l'(t-t_i)] = 0.$$

Whence, rearranging terms and setting $w_i = W_i'(t_i)$, etc., the first-order condition is

$$\frac{w_i - w_l}{w_i - w_l - f_i} = -\frac{pU'(X_a)}{(1-p)U'(X_b)}.$$

The term on the right-hand side represents the individual's marginal rate of substitution of wealth in state (*a*), X_a, for wealth in state (*b*), X_b, given the probability of being in either state, or, alternatively, the slope of an indifference curve in (X_a, X_b) space. The term on the left-hand side represents the marginal rate at which X_a can be transformed into X_b by reallocating the time budget from legitimate to illegitimate activities. The choice situation is shown in Figure 1. The outcome is certain only when the individual devotes his entire time to legitimate activity, that is $W_i(0)=0$, $F_i(0)=0$ and $X_a = X_b = W + W_l(t)$. The situation of specialisation in legiti-

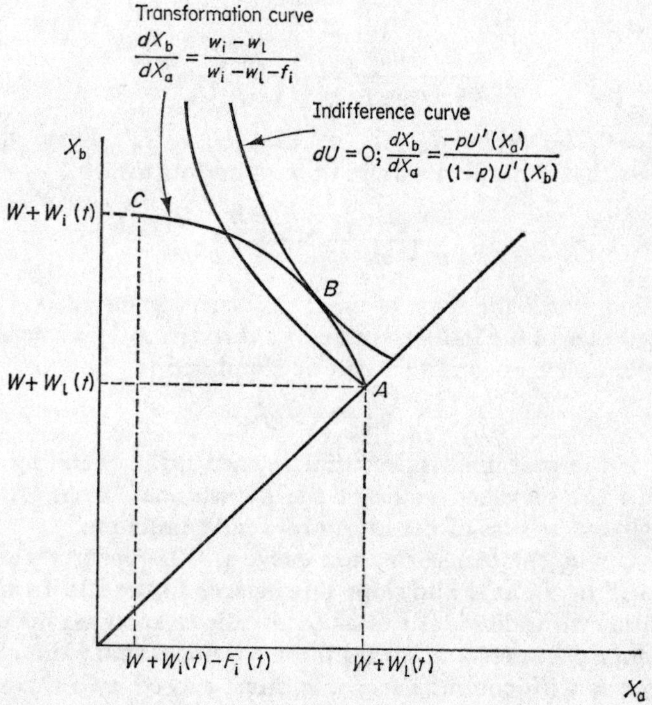

FIG. 1

mate activity is characterised by $X_a = X_b$, a condition which is met only on a ray of 45° from the origin.

The situation where an individual commits no crimes is represented by A, where the transformation curve meets the certainty line, that is $t_i = 0$. The situation where the individual specialises in criminal activity is represented by point C, where $X_a = W + W_i(t) - F_i(t)$ and $X_b = W + W_i(t)$. $X_a \lesseqgtr 0$ as $F_i(t) \gtreqless W + W_i(t)$, but we shall assume that $X_a > 0$. Since at A all time is devoted to legitimate activity, the transformation curve is not defined to the right of that point; likewise it is not defined to the left of C.

In the conditions outlined above a sufficient condition for participation in illegitimate activity is

$$\left.\frac{dEU}{dt_i}\right|_{t_i=0} > 0,$$

that is

$$\frac{w_i - w_l}{w_i - w_l - f_i} > -\frac{pU_a'}{(1-p)U_b'}.$$

At $t_i = 0$, however, $X_a = X_b$ so that $U_a' = U_b'$. From this it follows that the sufficient condition amounts to

$$\frac{w_i - w_l}{w_i - w_l - f_i} > -\frac{p}{1-p}.$$

In other words the slope of the transformation curve at A must exceed that of the indifference curve through A. It is interesting to note that this condition can be simplified to

$$w_i - w_l > pf_i,$$

that is the marginal differential reward from offending must exceed the expected value of the punishment, irrespective of the characteristics of the utility-of-wealth function.

If $w_l > w_i$ the transformation curve will be positively sloped but will begin at A and slope downwards to the left. In such a situation an individual would be unable to increase his utility by moving from A and would therefore not offend. This clearly conforms with common sense: w_i must exceed w_l if there is to be any attraction in offending to balance the penalty if caught.

If $f_i < w_i - w_l$ the transformation curve is again positively sloped, but in this case begins at A and slopes upwards to the right, thus inducing specialisation in offending. Even if capture is certain ($p = 1$) the marginal differential reward from offending outweighs the value of the punishment (see also Chapter 7, p. 63).

Arguably, the standard and certainly the most interesting case, however, is where $w_i > w_l$ and $f_i > w_i - w_l$. This entails that the numerator of the expression for the slope is negative, the case illustrated in Figure 1. It should be noted that our earlier assumptions that W_i'', $W_l'' < 0$, $F_i'' > 0$ ensure a transformation curve concave to the origin and we shall take this to be a feature of the standard case.

OFFENDERS' REACTIONS TO CHANGES IN THE VARIABLES

If society is to lessen the number of offences, it must be done by alteration of one or more of the variables on which the supply of offences depends, namely p, f_i, w_i and w_l. Common sense would suggest that rises in p, f_i and w_l would lower the level of offences, as would a fall in w_i. Let us see whether this is really so.

(a) An Increase in the Probability of Punishment

If we assume the utility of wealth to be an increasing function of wealth itself, that is $U'(X) > 0$, then it follows that $U'(X_a)$ and $U'(X_b)$ are both positive. Since p is positive, all the elements of the expression for the slope of an indifference curve,

$$-\frac{pU_a'}{(1-p)U_b'},$$

are positive, and it follows from the negative sign that the slope is negative. A rise in p will increase the numerator and reduce the denominator, thus increasing the absolute value of the slope. Since the transformation curve is unaffected by a change in p, the new equilibrium position must lie to the right of the initial position. A rise in p unequivocally reduces the level of offending. One minor qualification is that in the case of a corner solution

($t_i = t$) a large increase in p might be necessary to induce such whole-hogging offenders to enter legitimate activity at all.

(*b*) *An Increase in the Level of Punishment*

In the case of a rise in p, the result was obtained for indifference curves of negative slope. In this case the result depends on an additional property of indifference curves – their convexity or concavity to the origin. We shall first show that the properties of convexity and concavity are, respectively, associated with risk-avoidance and risk-preference.

An indifference curve will be convex to the origin if, starting from an endowment of (X_a^0, X_b^0), when the amount of X_a is reduced to X_a^1 and that of X_b increased to X_b^1 so as to leave the individual at the same level of utility as before, the slope at (X_a^1, X_b^1) is greater than at (X_a^0, X_b^0). (The reader may find it helpful to refer to Figure 1 at this point.) The slope of an indifference curve is given by

$$-\frac{pU_a'}{(1-p)U_b'}.$$

Recall that the value of p has been assumed not to vary with the values of X_a and X_b. Therefore, if the absolute value of the slope is to be greater in the new position (1) than in the old (0), we must have

$$\frac{U'(X_a^1)}{U'(X_b^1)} > \frac{U'(X_a^0)}{U'(X_b^0)}.$$

Now $U'(X)$ is the derivative or slope of the individual's utility-of-wealth schedule, of which a possible variant is depicted in Figure 2. Since (*a*) is the caught state and (*b*) the uncaught state, X_a is smaller than X_b by the value of $F_i(t_i)$ for any value of t_i. $U'(X_a)$ will exceed $U'(X_b)$ only if the utility-of-wealth function is concave from below, as in the diagram, and will be smaller only if the function is convex from below.

Now let us arbitrarily reduce the individual's endowment of X_a from X_a^0 to X_a^1. Then $U'(X_a^1) > U'(X_a^0)$. If X_b is now increased so as to equate *CD* with *AB* and therefore keep the individual at the same level of utility as before, then $U'(X_b^1) < U'(X_b^0)$. Hence if the utility-of-wealth function is concave from below ($U''(X) < 0$) then

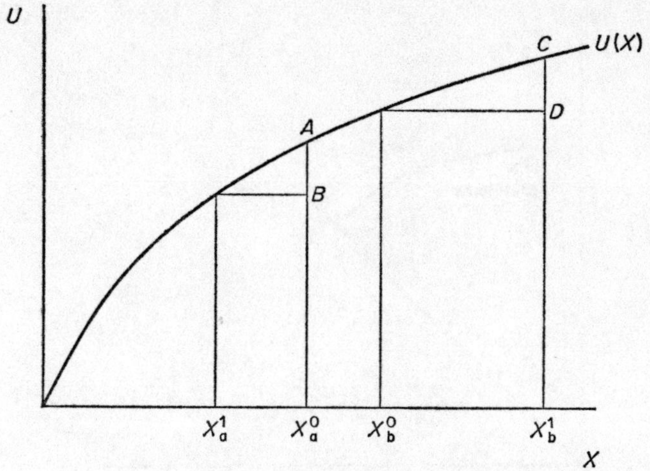

FIG. 2

$$\frac{U'(X_a^{\ 1})}{U'(X_b^{\ 1})} > \frac{U'(X_a^{\ 0})}{U'(X_b^{\ 0})},$$

that is the indifference curves are convex to the origin. By similar reasoning it can be shown that if the utility-of-wealth function is convex from below ($U''(X) > 0$) then the indifference curves are concave to the origin.

The feature $U''(X) < 0$ has the interesting property of being associated with aversion to risk, defined as rejection of a fair bet, one whose expected value is zero (for example a bet whereby you lose £1 if a coin falls heads, gain £1 if it falls tails). $U''(X) > 0$ is associated with risk-preference, defined as acceptance of a fair bet. For a fuller treatment, consult Green ([3], ch. 13, section 4).

We have now therefore established an association between concavity/convexity of indifference curves in (X_a, X_b) space and risk-preference/risk-aversion respectively.

We are now in a position to return to the main line of argument, namely how does the level of offences react to increases in the weight of punishment? An increase in the average and marginal punishment for all values of t_i reduces X_a while leaving X_b unchanged, since an increase in punishment does

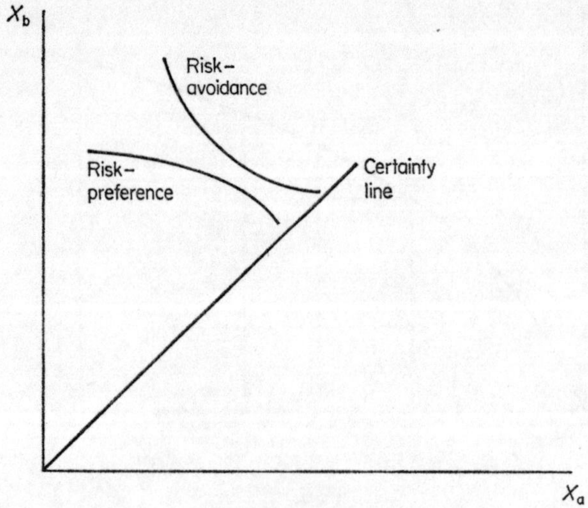

FIG. 3

not affect the uncaught state. At the original division of the offender's time, the slope of the indifference curve rises if he is risk-averse: if $X_a^1 < X_a^0$, then $U'(X_a^1) > U'(X_a^0)$ and

$$\frac{U'(X_a^1)}{U'(X_b^1)} > \frac{U'(X_a^0)}{U'(X_b^0)},$$

where $X_b^1 = X_b^0$ and therefore $U'(X_b^1) = U'(X_b^0)$. The transformation curve pivots downwards on A with the result that its slope is less at the original division of time than it was before. Since at that division of time the indifference curve is steeper and the transformation curve less steep, the offender will move towards the certainty line and spend less time in illicit activity.

For risk-preferrers $U'(X_a^1) < U'(X_a^0)$ and the same line of reasoning will show that at the original division of time both slopes are lower. Consequently it is not certain whether the offender will engage in less, more or the same amount of illicit activity. But although the possibility exists that a risk-preferrer might increase his offending in response to small increases in punishment, there will be a level of punishment beyond which even all risk-preferrers will opt for wholly legitimate activity.

An increase in the average level of punishment without an

increase in the marginal punishment ($F_i(t_i)/t_i$ rises but f_i does not) displaces the transformation curve horizontally by an equal distance throughout its length. Risk-avoiders would offend less and risk-preferrers might offend more in response to small increases, but all would eventually forsake criminal activity if the changes were large enough.

(*c*) *A Rise in the Average and Marginal Legitimate Reward,* $W_1(t-t_i)$, w_1

This will shift the transformation curve outwards at A but not at C. The transformation curve therefore pivots outwards on C. For any division of time, X_a and X_b increase by equal amounts. For risk-avoiders $U'(X_a{}^1) < U'(X_a{}^0)$, but it is also true that $U'(X_b{}^1) < U'(X_b{}^0)$, so that it is not clear whether

$$\frac{U'(X_a{}^1)}{U'(X_b{}^1)} > \frac{U'(X_a{}^0)}{U'(X_b{}^0)}$$

or not. In fact the slope of the indifference curve will be lower if the marginal utility-of-wealth function ($U'(X)$), which is downward-sloping ($U''(X) < 0$), is concave from below ($U'''(X) < 0$). It is therefore possible that, at the original division of time, a risk-avoider's indifference curve would have a lower slope. Therefore a rise in the average and marginal legitimate reward cannot be relied upon to impel risk-avoiders to reduce illicit activity. The same holds good for risk-preferrers. Since a necessary condition for an increase in illicit activity $U'''(X) < 0$ and since this is not a sufficient condition (because of the lowered slope of the transformation curve), it may be said that offending is likely to be reduced.

(*d*) *A Fall in the Average and Marginal Illicit Return,* $W_i(t_i)$, w_i

This pivots the transformation curve downwards on A, reducing X_a and X_b by equal amounts. Much the same analysis applies as for the previous case, except that here the necessary, but again not sufficient, condition for an increase in illicit activity is $U'''(X) > 0$. Again it seems safe to say that the change will reduce illicit activity.

If, however, there is a fall in the *differential* return from illicit activity – that is $(w_i - w_l)$ – at the point of equilibrium, the slope of the transformation curve falls by pivoting on the point of equilibrium and all offenders will reduce illicit activity.

As a qualification to cases (*c*) and (*d*), if there is specialisation in illicit activity, that is a corner solution, small changes in the variables may have no effect.

To summarise, only when the probability of capture is raised is it certain that no offender will increase the level of his offending and only those who specialise may not reduce it. The other attempts to reduce offending cannot be relied upon to achieve the desired result. This may perhaps be the rationale for the view that is sometimes heard that increases in the probability of conviction are more likely to reduce crime than other measures, notably increased punishment.

EHRLICH'S MODEL AND THEORIES OF CRIMINAL BEHAVIOUR

Before we go on to consider further problems involved in controlling the supply of offences it may be helpful to set the model into the context of theories of criminal behaviour generally. In particular, it should be noted that Ehrlich's model, with its emphasis on the probability of conviction, the weight of punishment and the level of differential returns, by no means precludes sociological, political, psycho-medical and physiological theories. Remember that w_i stands for all the returns from illicit activity and not only those for which money values can be established in some market, explicit or implicit. Consider the psychopath's unprovoked attack on an innocent bystander or the sadist's torture of a cat: it is possible that there is some bribe such individuals would accept to forgo particular acts or some payment they might be prepared to make to secure permission to perpetrate the act. The term 'psychic income' may be found useful where illicit activity affords direct satisfaction to offenders (for example murder, rape, 'senseless' violence, vandalism) rather than boosting their purchasing power. In general, it is perceived values of the variables that are important for individuals' decisions about illicit acts, even where these can be shown to diverge from actual values. The reader may care to consider one of the well-established theories of offending behaviour and work out what it asserts about offenders' perceived or actual p, f_i, w_i or w_l. The value of

Ehrlich's approach, however, consists not only in its ability to subsume the well-established theories but in its systematic admission of the possibility that offending may be a response to opportunity.

MANIPULATION OF THE VARIABLES – SOME DIFFICULTIES

It will be clear that the model does not imply that p and f are society's only decision variables. Increases in p have been shown, at worst, not to increase the level of offending. Increasing the amount of punishment per offence, apart from the difficulty that the number of offences may not be reduced, may be counterproductive in another way. Stigler [4] points out that the structure of punishments must be carefully planned so as to offer marginal deterrence to larger crimes. If the penalty for armed robbery is death, the offender might as well shoot as many potential witnesses as he conveniently can in the interests of lowering the probability of apprehension. This precept was ignored in medieval times when the practice of prescribing outlawing or hanging for comparatively minor crimes apparently reduces f to zero for subsequent offences, thereby creating an incentive, as Ehrlich's model would predict, for specialisation in illicit activity. (If f is truly zero then the transformation curve coincides with the certainty line between A and the value of $X_a(=X_b)$ at which all time is devoted to illicit activity.) But Stigler's example does not involve f falling to zero. In effect it is not like a season ticket bought at the beginning of the season, but being charged the season-ticket price when one is eventually caught trying to sneak in free. *Ex ante* the probability of capture for offence k is p and the punishment if caught is f_j, equal to the punishment for the most serious offence, j, yet committed, not the punishment for the offence k itself. Ehrlich notes that the practice of imposing concurrent sentences for several offences lowers the punishment per offence and therefore brings forth a greater supply of offences. But, as Stigler notes, if the probability of apprehension is p per offence, the chance of not having been caught after n offences is $(1-p)^n$ and this expression tends to zero as n

becomes large. Therefore the fact of a fixed cost or season ticket for offences does not preclude a measure of marginal deterrence.

Again, the influence of f will be perverse if the offender does not attach a negative value to the punishment. There could be several reasons for this, for example inadequate personalities may enjoy the security and comradeship of prison life as well as the regular well-cooked meals.

Operation on w_i and w_l may involve agencies outside the criminal justice system proper. Society can seek to increase w_l by creating job skills in (actual or potentially identifiable) offenders, reducing unemployment and so on. Furthermore, legitimate outlets for frustration, aggression and the love of risk can be created through provision for risky recreational pursuits and opportunities for adventure, for example in the armed forces. In certain large Japanese business concerns a room is set aside where employees are free to flog effigies of their bosses, the aim being to reduce the gap of w_i over w_l. w_i can be reduced through controls on firearms, depriving offenders of the proceeds of their wrong-doing and, less directly, by redistribution of wealth and other measures to reconcile the disenchanted with the society within which they live.

DETERRENCE AND REFORM

In the one-period model expounded above, a potential offender is postulated to respond to the expected utility of a two-state choice. The emphasis is explicitly on deterrence of criminal behaviour. But it is generally acknowledged that an important objective of the C.J.S. is to alter the future careers of those who are exposed to it. Again, the ways in which it does so can be classified according to the effects on offenders' p, f, w_i and w_l in subsequent periods.

The C.J.S. may raise p; the fact of having been caught makes it easier for the authorities to catch one next time. The C.J.S. may serve to raise perceived f or lower it through being less or more congenial than expected. By rehabilitation the C.J.S. may increase w_l; by exposure to fellow prisoners offenders may increase their w_i through acquisition of illicit skills or formation of unwholesome associations. The very fact of having a criminal record will restrict employment opportunities and thereby reduce w_l. Preventive detention can be regarded as a way of ensuring that $w_i = 0$ for a number of periods.

FURTHER COMPLICATIONS – A CONVEX TRANSFORMATION CURVE

So far we have confined attention to the case where diminishing returns renders the transformation curve concave. However, it is possible that, due to economies of specialisation for example, there might be increasing marginal returns in both legitimate and illegitimate activity. With a convex transformation curve, risk-preferrers will specialise in either kind of activity; risk-avoiders might mix their activities.

It is interesting to work through the effects of changes in the control variables for this case:

(1) An increase in p unequivocally either reduces illicit activity or does not affect it.

(2) An increase in the average and marginal value of punishment causes risk-preferrers either totally to abandon crime or has no effect. This is a change from the case of a concave transformation curve. Risk-avoiders will either offend less or not change.

(3) An increase in the average and marginal legitimate return will induce risk-preferrers either to switch to wholly legitimate use of time or have no effect. Risk-avoiders who specialise in offending will either not change or will reduce their offending, possibly totally. For risk-avoiders who are part-time offenders, the condition $U'''(X) < 0$ is necessary for an increase in offending but not sufficient; if $U'''(X) \geqslant 0$ they will offend less.

(4) With a decrease in average and marginal illicit return, risk-preferrers will either switch completely or not at all and risk-avoiders specialising in offending will offend less. For risk-avoiders who are part-time offenders, $U'''(X) > 0$ is a necessary condition for an increase in offending but not sufficient; if $U'''(X) \leqslant 0$ they will offend less.

2 The Socially Optimal Level of Offences

We saw in the last chapter how the level of offences responded to changes in society's control variables. In this chapter the problem of minimising the social loss from offending will be explored.

In Chapter 1 our concern was with the utility-maximising behaviour of one agent in the system, namely the offender. Here the losses the rest of society sustains as a result of crime are explicitly recognised. Let us set down the various parties' gains and losses.

(1) Offenders gain through the excess of W_i over W_1 and lose through exposure to the correction process, F_i, with a probability p.

(2) Victims suffer directly by (*a*) losing those goods stolen from them or by having 'bads' inflicted upon them; it is reasonable to suppose that their losses are, in general, related negatively to offenders' gains, notably where theft is involved; (*b*) indirectly, by incurring an opportunity cost in taking precautions in order to prevent offences against person or property.

(3) Society collectively devotes resources to a criminal justice system (C.J.S.) which detects, apprehends, punishes and rehabilitates offenders, the justification being that the social loss from offences prevented by the C.J.S. exceeds the system's costs.

It is plain, then, that there is a number of elements which together make up the social loss from offending. The C.J.S. has two main variables which can be manipulated to reduce the level of social loss, namely p, the probability of conviction and f, the amount of punishment per offence.

In his pioneering article Becker [2] formulates an expression which relates social loss to the level of offences, with p and f as control variables. In the interests of expounding this model in the simplest possible way, questions about establishing the welfare significance of certain categories of loss are left as open as possible. These questions are of course important and controversial and we set them aside only to reactivate them later. The aim is to derive results acceptable on the widest variety of views as to welfare significance.

There are three distinct items of social loss.

(1) The direct value of loss from offences, D, which is related to the number of offences, O: $D=D(O)$. In Becker's formulation, D is the balance of victims' loss less offenders' gain.

(2) Police and court costs of detecting and apprehending offenders, C, are related to the number of offences and the probability of conviction: for a given level of O it involves additional cost to raise p; to maintain a given level of p with an increased level of O also involves additional cost, that is $C=C(p, O)$.

(3) The social costs of punishment depend on the number of offences, O, on the probability of conviction, p, and on the value to the convict of the punishment per offence. Let b be a factor which converts subjective costs, f, to social costs. The total social cost of punishment is therefore $bpfO$.

This b factor may seem rather mysterious. It is, however, a most useful device to enable results to be derived without the need for prior consideration of questions as to whose gains and losses are to count and how much. To illustrate the role of b, here are two examples. The first is Becker's own. If the punishment is a fine, f will be equal to the fine. But fines are transfers from convicts to the remainder of society. Hence the net social loss is nil, and $b=0$. The punishment costs society as a whole nothing. Or take a second example. If we say that prisoners' subjective valuations of loss of freedom are to count, and that the costs of imprisonment in the sense of buildings, staff and so on amount to $f/10$ then $b=1 \cdot 1$. If, however, it is decided that prisoners' subjective valuations are not to count, then $b=0 \cdot 1$. The result derived below remains valid whatever the value of b.

The total loss from crime, L, is the sum of these three elements, that is

$$L=D(O)+C(p, O)+bpfO.$$

Minimisation of L with respect to the control variables p and f entails partial differentiation of L with respect to each in turn and setting the resulting expressions equal to zero:

$$\frac{\partial L}{\partial f}=D'\frac{\partial O}{\partial f}+C'\frac{\partial O}{\partial f}+bpf\frac{\partial O}{\partial f}+bpO=0$$

and

$$\frac{\partial L}{\partial p}=D'\frac{\partial O}{\partial p}+C'\frac{\partial O}{\partial p}+\frac{\partial C}{\partial p}+bpf\frac{\partial O}{\partial p}+bfO=0.$$

Becker recasts these expressions to incorporate the elasticity of offences with respect to p and f, e_p and e_f, equal respectively to $-(p/O)(\partial O/\partial p)$ and $-(f/O)(\partial O/\partial f)$. This is brought about by transferring the final two terms in each equation to the right-hand side, dividing through by $\partial O/\partial f$ and $\partial O/\partial p$ respectively, taking $-bpf$ as a factor on the right-hand side and rearranging terms. The following expressions can be obtained:

$$e_f=\frac{bpf}{D'+C'+bpf}$$

and

$$e_p=\frac{bpf}{D'+C'+\frac{\partial C}{\partial p}\bigg/\frac{\partial O}{\partial p}+bpf}.$$

Since all the terms in the expression for e_f are positive it follows that the denominator exceeds the numerator. Therefore, at the optimum, $e_f<1$. Turning now to the expression for e_p, we know that $\partial C/\partial p$ is positive and $\partial O/\partial p$ negative. The denominator of the expression for e_p is less than that in the expression for e_f. Hence a necessary condition for minimising the social loss from offences is $e_p>e_f$. Note, however, that this is a necessary and not a sufficient condition. The condition might be satisfied where, for example $\partial L\partial/f=\partial L/\partial p\neq 0$, a situation in which social loss is not at a minimum. The most that can be said is that if $e_p\leqslant e_f$, then it is certain that loss is not being minimised. That would imply that if a change is to be made in the level of expenditure on the C.J.S., f should be increased *relative to p*. But if $e_f>1$, the right policy is to increase spending on f.

Now it can be shown that the condition $e_p > e_f$ is satisfied if and only if p and f are such that crime does not pay, that is, in Ehrlich's terms [1], $w_i - w_l < pf_i$. This result is established in the Appendix to this chapter.

Notice that this result has been obtained using weak assumptions. All that is required is that D', C',$(\partial C/\partial p)$, $b, p, f, O > 0$ and $\partial O/\partial p$, $\partial O/\partial f < 0$. The result can therefore be said to have a high degree of generality. In particular, it has not been necessary even to enumerate the content of b, let alone value its elements. The same is true of D': there has been no need to discuss whether victims' and offenders' gains and losses should all be counted, whether offenders' opportunity costs should be counted or the resources potential victims devote to self-protection.

The next three chapters develop the present chapter in three main ways.

(1) In the next chapter we take a look at empirical work on the actual effectiveness of the C.J.S. The question is, should more resources be devoted to the C.J.S. and what is the optimum mode of deployment of a given level of resources?

(2) In Chapter 4 we will discuss the very questions of enumeration and evaluation of gains and losses that were firmly set aside in the present chapter.

(3) Chapter 5 examines the question of sub-optimisation, where, for example, f can be varied but not p, or p but not f.

APPENDIX

The purpose of this appendix is to show that the condition $e_p > e_f$ is satisfied if and only if crime does not pay, that is $w_i - w_l < pf_i$.

For present purposes, e_p and e_f are defined with respect to the offender's utility-maximising amount of time spent in illicit activity, t_i^*, and not the level of offences, O. Thus

$$e_p = -\frac{\partial t_i^*}{\partial p} \cdot \frac{p}{t_i^*}$$

and

$$e_f = -\frac{\partial t_i^*}{\partial f} \cdot \frac{f}{t_i^*}.$$

The condition is equivalent to

$$\frac{\partial t_i^*}{\partial p} \cdot p > \frac{\partial t_i^*}{\partial f} \cdot f.$$

To evaluate these partial derivatives, we use the chain rule, that is

$$\frac{\partial t_i^*}{\partial p} = \frac{\partial t_i^*}{\partial \frac{(dEU)}{(dt_i)}} \cdot \frac{\partial \frac{(dEU)}{(dt_i)}}{\partial p}$$

and similarly for $\partial t_i^* / \partial f$, where $dEU/dt_i (=0)$ is the first-order condition for a utility maximum.

Now it can be said that the condition is fulfilled if

$$\frac{\partial \frac{(dEU)}{(dt_i)}}{\partial p} \cdot p > \frac{\partial \frac{(dEU)}{(dt_i)}}{\partial f} \cdot f.$$

That is we must differentiate the first-order condition with respect to p and f.

The first-order condition is

$$K = p(w_i - w_l - f) + (1 - p)\lambda(w_i - w_l) = 0,$$

where $\lambda = U'(X_b)/U'(X_a)$. Now,

$$\frac{\partial K}{\partial p} = (w_i - w_l - f) - \lambda(w_i - w_l)$$

and

$$\frac{\partial K}{\partial f} = -p.$$

The condition is therefore fulfilled if

$$p((1 - \lambda)(w_i - w_l) - f) > -pf.$$

If $\lambda = 1$ then the left-hand side equals $-pf$. The condition is fulfilled only if $\lambda > 1$, that is if $U'(X_b) > U'(X_a)$. Since $X_b > X_a$, this will be true only if $U'' > 0$, that is all offenders are risk-preferrers.

What must the relationship between the variables be if risk-avoiders are not to be offenders? Since risk-avoiders' indifference curves are convex to the origin and the transformation curve is concave, the condition

$$\left.\frac{dEU}{dt_i}\right|_{t_i=0} > 0$$

is a necessary condition for entry into illegitimate activity though, of course, only a sufficient condition for risk-preferrers. Therefore, if this expression is less than or equal to zero, that is sufficient to deter risk-avoiders since

$$\frac{w_i - w_l}{w_i - w_l - f} \leqslant -\frac{p}{1-p},$$

that is

$$w_i - w_l \leqslant pf.$$

3 The Effectiveness of the Criminal Justice System (C.J.S.)

In order to assess the effectiveness of the C.J.S., it is necessary to quantify two relationships: (*a*) the responsiveness of the supply of offences to the various control variables, and (*b*) the relationship between expenditure and these variables. In this chapter we shall be looking at three studies which throw light on these questions, two from the United States and one from the United Kingdom.

The first is Ehrlich's attempt to test and quantify the model outlined in Chapter 1 of the present volume [1]. It will be recalled that, in general, the supply of offences was postulated to depend on the return from illicit activity, the return from lawful activity, the amount of punishment if caught and the probability of capture. The supply-of-offences function can be summarised as

$$\frac{Q}{N} = f(P, F, Y_i, Y_l, U, V, Z). \qquad (3.1)$$

Q/N is the rate of occurrence per annum of some particular crime per head of the population in the states of the United States. P is the probability of conviction and F the amount of punishment per crime. Because of inadequate data it is impossible to obtain ideal measures of Y_i and Y_l – illegitimate and legitimate return. It is of course impossible to measure the potential criminal's subjective valuations of these returns. As a proxy for Y_i, Ehrlich adopts the variable W, the level of transferable assets in a state, and that, in turn, is approximated by the observable variable, the median family income of a state, on the grounds that the higher the income the more there is likely to be worth stealing. A measure of legitimate opportunity is X, the percentage of families below half the median income in a state, the reasoning being that if that figure is high, there is a large number of people who have little to lose by using their time in illegal as opposed to legal employments. U is the rate of unemployment, V is a set of environmental variables and Z summarises the effect of non-quantifiable variables. Only the seven U.S. 'index' crimes – murder, rape, assault, burglary, larceny, robbery and auto theft, all punishable by imprisonment – are considered. This fact makes for a convenient measure of P – the ratio of offenders imprisoned to offences known – and a good proxy for F – the time spent in prison, T. Note that the use of this measure obviates the need to evaluate F in money terms.

The second equation in the system is necessary because although Q/N depends upon P, P is likely to depend also upon Q/N. Another important determinant of P is no doubt the law enforcement agencies' level of expenditure per head, E/N. But it is reasonable to suppose that the higher the rate of crime, the lower the productivity of expenditure per head in achieving P, or, what is the same thing, the higher the cost of attaining a given level of P. The following production function is therefore postulated:

$$P = B(E/N)^{\beta_1}(Q/N)^{\beta_2}Z, \tag{3.2}$$

where B is a constant and Z is a set of environmental variables affecting productivity.

The principal results of the analysis are that the rate of crime in each category varies inversely with the probability of imprisonment and the length of time served – p and f in the theoretical model. Property crimes vary positively with X and W, or, in terms of their theoretical counterparts, property crime is high were w_i is high and where w_1 is low. Crimes against the person show no great sensitivity to X and W.

It will be recalled that Ehrlich's original formulation was cast in terms of the expected utility of a criminal prospect bearing a certain value of punishment if caught and a certain probability of capture. Manipulation of p and f is envisaged to have only a deterrent effect. In the empirical work, however, the elasticities of response with respect to P and T include also the preventive effects of detention. This can be shown to be related to the seriousness of the crime: the rate of offences is inversely related to the expected time in prison per offence (PT) and since PT is greater for the more serious crimes (that is those against the person) the preventive effect is greater for these. The conclusion is that not only is the calculated elasticity of response of crimes against the person with respect to P and T small, but part of that captures the preventive effect. Doubt is therefore cast on the deterrent effect of imprisonment for such crimes.

But perhaps the most interesting feature of Ehrlich's system is that it is possible to estimate the marginal effectiveness of the C.J.S. The first equation relates the rate of crime to, among other variables, the probability of imprisonment:

$$\log \frac{Q}{N} = b_1 \log P + \dots . \tag{3.3}$$

The second equation relates the probability of imprisonment to the crime rate and the expenditure on the law-enforcement agencies:

$$\log P = \beta_1 \log \frac{E}{N} + \beta_2 \log \frac{Q}{N} + \dots . \tag{3.4}$$

Substituting for P in equation (3.3) yields

$$\log \frac{Q}{N} = b_1 \left(\beta_1 \log \frac{E}{N} + \beta_2 \log \frac{Q}{N} + \dots \right) + \dots . \tag{3.5}$$

The elasticity of the crime rate with respect to the rate of expenditure on the system is given by $\frac{d \log (Q/N)}{d \log (E/N)}$. Differentiating equation (3.5) with respect to $\log (E/N)$ therefore gives

$$\frac{d \log (Q/N)}{d \log (E/N)} = b_1\beta_1 + b_1\beta_2 \frac{d \log (Q/N)}{d \log (E/N)} . \tag{3.6}$$

Whence,

$$\frac{d \log (Q/N)}{d \log (E/N)} = \frac{b_1\beta_1}{1 - b_1\beta_2} . \tag{3.7}$$

Note that by expressing equations (3.3) and (3.4) in logarithmic form, it has not been necessary to consider all the variables influencing Q/N and P, since most are eliminated in calculating the elasticity of Q/N with respect to E/N.

Ehrlich's analysis produced the following regression results: $b_1=0\cdot991$, $\beta_1=0\cdot305$ and $\beta_2=-0\cdot908$. The elasticity of Q/N with respect to E/N is therefore -3. This means that a 1 per cent change in law-enforcement expenditure produces a 3 per cent change in the crime rate.

In 1965 the total expenditure on police and courts (E/N) in the United States was \$3·178 billion, of which 1 per cent was \$32 million. The President's Commission for Law Enforcement's 1965 estimate of the total social loss from the crime (other than expenditure on law enforcement) was \$5·986 billion. (For property crime, the value of what is stolen or destroyed is taken as the social cost; for crimes against the person, social cost is taken as the loss of earnings to the victim. In Chapter 4 the problems involved in valuing these costs will be discussed more fully.) This \$32 million increase in spending on the police and courts will thus produce a 3 per cent fall in the number of crimes and, presumably, in their social cost. This amounts to \$180 million (3 per cent of \$5·986 billion). It appears therefore that the marginal benefit–cost ratio of such expenditures is roughly 6 : 1.

The matter does not quite end there however. The proportion of the population jailed, C/N, is equal by definition to $P(Q/N)$. By substituting into equation (3.4),

$$\log\frac{C}{N}=\beta_1\log\frac{E}{N}+(\beta_2+1)\log\frac{Q}{N}+\ldots. \qquad (3.8)$$

From this the elasticity of C/N with respect to E/N can be found, that is

$$\frac{d\log\dfrac{C}{N}}{d\log\dfrac{E}{N}}=\beta_1=0\cdot305.$$

The net effects of a change in expenditure on police and courts on the expenditure on prisons is a combination of the two effects: the percentage reduction in the rate of flow of offences, e, plus the percentage increase in the number of offenders imprisoned through the rise in P, β_1. A 1 per cent rise in spending on the police and courts induces a change in the expenditure of prisons of $(\beta_1 + e)$ per cent $= (0 \cdot 305 - 3 \cdot 01)$ per cent $= -2 \cdot 7$ per cent. Expenditure on state and adult penal institutions in 1965 was \$385 million. A 1 per cent increase in spending on police and courts would reduce this by \$385 million $\times 0 \cdot 027 =$ \$10 million. The 1 per cent increase in spending on police and courts now appears to involve only a \$32 million − \$10 million = \$22 million increase in spending on the C.J.S. as a whole. The marginal benefit–cost ratio of public spending on the C.J.S. now appears to be 8 : 1. Of course, caution must be exercised in deriving results of this kind in view of, for example (*a*) the finding that there is only a $0 \cdot 6$ probability that $e > 0$, and (*b*) the crudeness of the valuation procedures.

It is interesting to note that the above analysis assumes an unchanged length of sentence. We can, however, investigate the marginal effectiveness of such an increase, on a *ceteris paribus* assumption. Ehrlich's estimates for all offences indicated that the elasticity of Q/N with respect to T was $-1 \cdot 123$. A 1 per cent increase in sentence length costing \$385 million $\times 0 \cdot 01 =$ \$4 million will reduce the social cost of crime by $1 \cdot 123$ per cent or \$5986 million $\times 0 \cdot 01123 =$ \$67 million. The marginal benefit–cost ratio of lengthening sentences is therefore 17 : 1.

While Ehrlich's model potentially answers the question, how much (more or less) should be spent on the police, the study by Chapman, Hirsch and Sonenblum [5] enables us (*a*) to identify which of the various police inputs (if any) should be increased, although in a restricted setting, and (*b*) to measure changes in police productivity over time.

The first step is to set up a regression with 'index' property crimes as the dependent variable. The choice of independent variables is conditioned by assumptions shared with Ehrlich's approach, that the offence rate is potentially sensitive to legitimate and illegitimate return. Different proxies are used. Race and length of education are used as proxies for legitimate income, the value of community real property for illegitimate return. The potential offender's perception of the chances of apprehension are postulated to be related to the change in crime rates from year to year: if, as has indeed been the case, the crime rate is increasing, potential offenders are supposed to conclude that police effectiveness is low.

Two less obvious explanatory variables are also used. The number of persons per household is thought to reduce the illicit return, since the more who live in a dwelling the less likely it is to be unoccupied at any given time. Furthermore, the higher the value of this variable, the higher the proportion of young children in the population, and children are less likely to commit index crimes. The level of population of each area is included to allow the possibility of a non-proportional relationship between population and crime.

There are eighty-two observations comprising Californian cities *excepting Los Angeles* in 1960. The variables found to be significant are number in household, median years of education, the change in the crime rate from the previous year and, not surprisingly, population.

Now we come to the second step. The regression equation is now used to predict the number of property crimes in Los Angeles for the years 1956–70. The reported number of property crimes was found to be consistently higher than the predicted number. An index of prevented crime is taken to be the ratio of predicted to reported crimes. A decline in this ratio over time is taken as a fall in police output. Since the ratio fell from 0·557 in 1956 to 0·279 in 1970, a fall in output is deemed to have occurred.

A widely used index of police output is the arrest rate. But its use as an output measure has the drawback that arrests are not necessarily a good thing since they can be cheaply generated at the expense of the conviction rate. Moreover, for many traffic offences, arrest is the only method of report. However, since this is not true of theft, larceny, robbery and vehicle theft, the arrest rate for these offences is used in an output measure.

The output measure is taken as a combination of the prevention rate and the arrest rate, specifically the sum of their weighted logarithms. A range of weights, always summing to unity, is used to produce a single output measure, since the authors feel unable to say what society's relative weights might be. In Chapter 6 the prevention value of detections is discussed.

In estimating the police-service production function, advantage is taken of the complementarity relating particular types of capital and labour input. For example, it is of no interest to try to assess separately the influence of a motor-cycle and its rider. Inputs are measured as the number of employees in each of four classes: motor-cycle teams, field officers, non-field officers and civilian employees.

Two conditions-of-service variables are introduced. The larger the number of ex-convicts in the community the easier it will be to make arrests, but the harder to prevent crime. A dummy variable separates the years after 1965 from those before, large-scale rioting in that year (it is conjectured) having brought about a permanent increase in the difficulty of crime prevention.

Since a log-linear relationship is hypothesised, coefficients represent the elasticity of output with respect to the various inputs. There are fifteen observations corresponding to the years 1956–70.

The salient results are these. The effect of motor-cycle teams on output is positive, significant and increases with the weight of prevention in output, but is not significant where output is measured solely by arrest rate. This result conforms with the view that since patrols are visible, their effect is more likely to be deterrent. Non-field officers appear to have a negative effect on output, except where the latter is measured by the arrest rate. The coefficient for civilian employees is positive and significant but rises with the weight assigned to prevention in the output measure. The two conditions-of-service variables are significant and their signs are as expected.

Provided that the police are good at allocating their own resources, whichever measure of output gives the best fit in the regression on the various independent variables must be taken as the measure they themselves adopt, even if they do so tacitly. The answer appears to be the arrest rate uncombined with preventions.

It is interesting to note that the coefficients that are significant and of the expected sign have values ranging from just under 2 to just over 4, depending on the relative weight assigned to preventions, for example a 1 per cent increase in motor-cycle teams would increase output by 2·82 per cent where preventions receive twice the weight of arrests. There is therefore some agreement with Ehrlich's result that elasticity of output with respect to input is 3. However, the major result of the study by Chapman *et al.* appears to be that a transfer of non-field officers to field duties of 1 per cent of the total would, if the present totals of the two categories were equal, increase output by 8 per cent without additional cost.

The study by Carr-Hill and Stern [6] in England and Wales covers some of the same ground as Ehrlich's, but there are interesting differences. The first equation relates to the supply of offences. The dependent variable is the number of offences *per capita* reported in a district; the explanatory variables are probability of apprehension (the clear-up rate), the number of policemen per head, the amount of capital per man, a punishment index (the proportion of convicts jailed) and the potential gains from offending (measured by the property-tax base). In addition, there are variables reflecting age composition and socio-economic factors.

In the second equation, the production function, the clear-up rate is the dependent variable, the explanatory variables being the number of policemen *per capita*, the proportion of offences that are violent (these are easier to clear up), an index of the size of the district, and a socio-economic indicator.

The third relates to the demand for policemen. The explanatory variables are the offence rate, the clear-up rate, the crime mix, the proportion of the population that is middle class, and population density.

The data base is a set of police districts in 1961 and 1966. In the supply-of-offences equation, the severity of punishment is negative and significant in both years. The same is true of the clear-up rate. The variable intended to capture illegitimate returns has a positive and significant effect in both years. The results therefore confirm Ehrlich's theory of offending behaviour. The elasticity of the offence rate with respect to the clear-up rate exceeds the elasticity with respect to the percentage of convicts jailed.

The elasticity of the offence rate with respect to the percentage of convicts jailed is 0·28 in 1961 and 0·17 in 1966, thus satisfying the necessary condition for an optimal value of f that $e_f < 1$. With such low figures, it is unlikely that an increase in f would produce a net benefit. The authors say that in order to effect a reduction of 1 per cent in the offence rate in 1966, an increase in the prison population of nearly 6 per cent would be required, since only 20 per cent of offenders were jailed in that year. The ratio of total costs of crime to those of imprisonment would have to exceed 6 : 1 if it were to be worthwhile to reduce crime by this method. What the ratio actually is it is impossible to say, since there is no estimate of the social loss from offences in England and Wales to compare with those Ehrlich uses for the United States, though recall that the ratio there was greater than 15 : 1 (see p. 32). Clearly, if this figure applied to England and Wales, an increase in the proportion jailed would be worthwhile.

With respect to the effectiveness of expenditure on p, it is not possible to repeat for England and Wales what Ehrlich does for the United States, because in the production-function equation the number of policemen per head has a significant and rather large (elasticity > 1) but negative effect. The authors account for this discouraging result by identifying three ways in which the number of policemen per head might affect the clear-up rate: (1) the offences they prevent may be the easiest to clear up – this would lower the clear-up rate; (2) there may be a tendency for the public to report certain offences (minor thefts for example) which in the absence of a policeman might go unreported because victims despair of a successful outcome – these would therefore be more difficult to clear up; and (3) a policeman in seeing and reporting a minor offence which otherwise would not be reported raises the clear-up rate.

In this chapter our main concern has been to extract from the three empirical studies money measures of the benefits and costs of manipulating C.J.S. variables, p and f. But it would be wrong to end the chapter without drawing attention to other methods of reducing social loss from crime. For example, in Ehrlich's results the elasticity of crimes against the person with respect to W (median family income, the proxy for illicit return) and X (the percentage of families below half median income, the proxy for legitimate opportunity) is in both cases positive and significant – 1·0458 and 0·9145 respectively – for property crime only, 2·3345 and 2·0547 – and for all crime, 2·0651 and 1·8013. A 1 per cent reduction in X will cause a fall of $108 million in the social loss from crime. This reduction could be brought about by a straight transfer from those above half median income to those below. Cost is zero, except for excess burden and administration. There are two objections to such a policy. For some, it may smack of danegeld. But, more importantly, X is being used as a proxy for legitimate opportunity. It could be argued that transfer payments do not of themselves improve opportunity for legitimate employment, but merely compensate for the lack of it. If the reduction in X were to be brought about by provision of additional or higher-paid employment, the cost would be that of diversion of jobs from other areas or groups of workers. An attempt to quantify this loss, or even to specify what it would be conceptually correct to measure, lies outside the scope of this book. On the other hand, unemployment itself is found to have an insignificant effect on crime rates. Perhaps, then, the straight transfer method would be successful. Finally, however, it is possible that X captures the effect of unemployment, and, if this is so, the straight transfer method does not seem such an attractive prospect.

4 The Valuation of Offences

Up to this point our policy has been to develop results using the absolute minimum number of assumptions regarding the social valuation of changes in criminal activity. In the preceding chapter, however, we were forced to modify this stance in order to explore the usefulness for policy of the empirical work under discussion. Our main concern in this chapter, then, is to enumerate and evaluate the gains and losses to society as a whole from these changes. We shall see that the question turns to a considerable extent on whose gains and losses are to count and how much.

THEFT

Since theft would seem to be the offence most readily susceptible to economic analysis, let us start with that. In evaluating the social loss from theft we are at once faced with the problem that since one party's loss is the other's gain, theft is a mere transfer involving no net loss to society as a whole, provided that society is defined to include all the relevant parties. The implication of this view is that the police should not waste resources trying to prevent theft, but should concentrate on other, socially harmful, offences. If a zero welfare significance is attached to offenders' gains, then the subjective value of what is stolen is an element of social loss from theft.

Tullock [7], however, points out that theft belongs to an important class of transactions which may be called 'contested transfers': even if offenders' gains were given full weight, social costs would arise because the potential parties to the transaction use their resources to contest the transfer.

Let us pursue this argument, considering first the offender. Shoup and Mehay [8] argue that the alternative income forgone by offenders is an important element in the social loss from theft. However, they say, since 'as some observers have pointed out, there is a strong empirical relationship between low income and the propensity to commit property crime, it may be that the typical thief's highest alternative earnings in legitimate activity are below those he can earn in crime'. This leads them to conclude that the amount stolen will overstate offenders' forgone legitimate earnings and therefore their opportunity costs. But there is another element in the cost to the offender of securing illegitimate earnings: the risk of capture and the subjective value of punishment. From Chapter 1 we know that the first-order condition for an offender to maximise utility is

$$\frac{w_i - w_l}{w_i - w_l - f} = -\frac{p}{(1-p)\lambda},$$

where, as in the Appendix to Chapter 2, $\lambda = U'(X_b)/U'(X_a)$. Rearranging terms,

$$w_i = w_l + \frac{pf}{p + \lambda - p\lambda}.$$

Interpreting the left-hand side as marginal gain from offending and the right-hand side as marginal cost, we see that for the risk-neutral person ($\lambda = 1$) the marginal cost of offending is equal to forgone legitimate earnings plus the expected value of punishment, or $w_l + pf$. For a risk-preferrer ($\lambda > 1$), marginal cost of offending is less because the weight attached to the expected value of punishment (that is $1/[p + \lambda - p\lambda]$) is less than unity. For a risk-avoider ($\lambda < 1$), of course, the weight attached to this expected value exceeds unity, but this is likely to be a less important case, for at all levels of p and f a risk-avoider will offend less than a risk-preferrer, particularly if p and f are so adjusted as to satisfy the necessary condition for minimising social loss that $pf > w_i - w_l$, that is crime does not pay, no risk-avoider will offend.

But the accuracy of forgone legitimate earnings as a measure of the opportunity costs of offending is not an important issue for the simple reason that what is stolen is an exact measure, at the margin. To assess the value of what is stolen can hardly be more difficult than to guess what an offender would have earned had he not been busy offending, together with his valuation of the prospect of punishment. However, if the punishment is by fine (a 'reverse theft'), the rest of society gains from the punishment exactly what the convict loses with the result that although the opportunity cost to the criminal includes pf, social opportunity cost does not. Suffice it to make a mental note that the possibility of a fine constitutes a reason why what is stolen, at the margin, might exceed the opportunity cost of stealing it, at the margin.

What we have said applies strictly at the margin. The presence of intra-marginal surplus for offenders would imply that the opportunity cost of theft as an aggregate is less than what is stolen. Becker [2], however, points out that if the crime 'industry' is competitive, this equality does hold in the aggregate. In the absence of barriers to entry (but think of the St Valentine's Day Massacre) or economies of scale, it does not seem likely that monopoly profit would long persist, though of course there may continue to be exceptionally gifted offenders whose services command an economic rent. Yet even if monopoly profit can be sustained by erecting barriers to entry, maintenance of these barriers will itself absorb resources. Tullock [7] points out that this is an important element of the misallocation of resources involved in monopoly, apart altogether from the 'distortion' of output.

No particular problem arises in connection with goods rather than money. Of course, those who actually steal the goods may not themselves be able to realise their full market value, though of course they may, for example if a smoker shoplifts cigarettes these will ge a good, even a perfect, substitute for cigarettes he would otherwise have had to buy; he therefore captures the full market value of his 'swag'. But if goods have to be 'fenced', they will have to be disposed of at a discount to compensate receivers for their time and risk. There is no reason to believe, however, that full market value is not captured by thieves and 'fences' taken together.

Even if we are prepared to countenance the view that both victims' and offenders' losses and gains are to count, victims may lose more than offenders gain when goods are stolen. The fact that a consumer retains a good rather than selling it is evidence that his valuation of the good exceeds that of the market. In other words, he enjoys consumers' surplus. The possibility that thieves might also derive consumers' surplus from stolen articles cannot be ruled out, but to enjoy this surplus they would have to retain the article, and since the article would be different from those currently available in legitimate markets – otherwise why would they derive surplus from it? – the consumers' surplus would be offset by increased risk of capture.

The important rule that emerges is that even if both victims' and offenders' losses are to count, it is worth at least the market value of what is stolen to prevent a theft. If offenders' gains are not to count it is worth twice the amount stolen to prevent a theft. If offenders are so far to be excluded from the definition of society that not even the costs of offending are to count, then the theft of goods amounts to their destruction and the value of preventing a theft again becomes equal to the value of what is (or would have been) stolen, plus unmeasurable surplus elements.

We now come to consider the other party to the contested transfer, namely the victims. There are three ways of reducing the expected value of loss through theft: self-insurance whereby the potential victim tries to reduce the *size* of his loss, for example by using time for leisure rather than for producing what is likely to be stolen; self-protection whereby the potential victim tries to reduce the *probability* of theft, for example by installing safes and burglar alarms; and market insurance whereby potential victims contribute to a pool, usually organised by a profit-seeking firm, from which those who lose are compensated, the idea being that it is preferable to lose a small amount with certainty than to risk a large loss. Ehrlich and Becker [9] develop a theory of demand for insurance in which the roles of these three forms of insurance are considered, and Carter [10] discusses the relationship between theft and insurance in the United Kingdom. Opportunity costs of market insurance itself are only those of administration, premia and claim settlements being transfers. However, insurers typically insist on certain standards of self-protection and self-insurance before accepting business, and these forms of protection do involve real costs.

The question is, what resources does the victim save if the level of crime is exogenously reduced? The utility-maximising potential victim will commit resources until the marginal reduction in expected value of loss is equal to the marginal cost of achieving it. But it is not easy to say how resource commitment would react to the postulated change. Perhaps it is safe to say that if the independent probability of loss from theft were to fall, the level of private resources devoted to loss prevention would fall too, but more than this it is impossible to say with any confidence.

VANDALISM

Offences involving damage or destruction are perhaps easier to value because there is no transfer element. The value of the offence is the value of the property destroyed. But whereas with thefts there is a presumption that offenders' costs will be close to the amount stolen, no similar link can be established with the amount of destruction. An important cost for a vandal is the expected value of punishment, but this is not necessarily related to the value of damage done.

But perhaps the absence of a transfer effect is more apparent than real. An act of vandalism is a direct conversion of equipment or property into utility, whereas the utilities derived from theft are often indirect and involve exchange of stolen articles into money followed by conversion of the latter into goods or services that do afford direct utility. And even some thefts involve direct conversion of objects into utility, for example the smoker who shoplifts cigarettes. The reason why it is not possible to postulate equality between the value of utility derived from vandalism (and therefore at most offenders' costs) and the market value of the article is that the market value is established for a use quite other than that to which the vandal puts the article. But is it possible to say whether the value of the utility a vandal derives from destroying an article exceeds or falls short of its market value? It would seem not.

Not that we are suggesting that the market value of an article is necessarily an exact or even a minimum measure of the social loss of what victims forgo. If vandals demolish an electricity pylon, an important cost is that of its re-erection. But while supplies are interrupted, customers are losing consumers' surplus. This loss may be considerable. However, if electricity is being sold at a price less than *MC*, that is with a subsidy, consumers lose *ABC* (see Figure 4). But the rest of society gains *EBCD*. Net loss to society as a whole is therefore *AEF*−*FCD*,

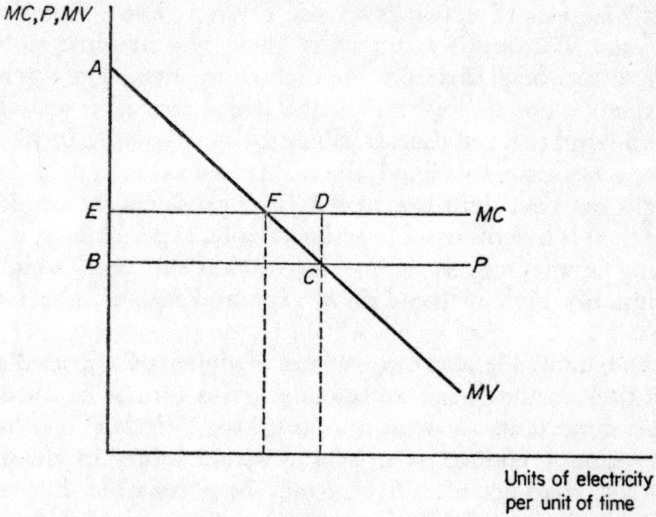

FIG. 4

considerably less than consumers' surplus. If the item is taxed, social loss will be greater than consumers' surplus.

Of course, the tempting solution to all these difficulties is to say that offenders' gains and losses should be set at nought, and that the loss from vandalism is the cost of rectifying the damage (at most).

VIOLENT CRIME

If a violent (or destructive) act is committed in the process of a robbery, whether to secure swag or expedite escape, only the loss to the victim need be considered, since for offenders we can continue to assume that, at the margin, the resources used and expected penalties are balanced against the amount stolen. Shoup and Mehay [8] deal with victims' loss by assimilating injury by criminal act to injury by road accident. This solution makes a strong appeal since it sanctions the use of standard figures for road-accident losses that are already formulated in most countries, so that no further analysis or measurement is needed. However, Shoup and Mehay adopt the cost of treatment plus loss of earnings as the relevant losses from traffic accidents. For injuries involving theft, the amount stolen is taken as the social loss from the theft component. For a genuine car theft – not a 'joy-ride' – the social loss is taken as the second-hand price of the car. Since for rape only slight physical injury is typically sustained, the rather low value appropriate to a slight road accident is assigned. This produces the result that a car theft is five times more serious than a rape. Plainly, what is lacking is an estimate of the warm-blooded costs, which are presumably high in the case of rape and low or zero for car thefts.

Rape, homicide and pure crimes of violence in general differ from theft in that what an offender gains cannot be measured in the same units as what a victim loses. Victims' loss has no ready money counterpart. Where actual injury or death are involved, road-accident figures may be acceptable. But crimes involving threats of violence cannot easily be assimilated to road accidents. The same is perhaps true of the fear, as opposed to the physical injury, undergone by those assaulted. Since it is not obvious how valuations of these 'bads' can be inferred from potential victims' actual trade-offs, the only apparent solution would seem to be to set up an experiment which places potential victims in simulated market situations in which they are faced with a hypothetical tariff whereby money can be traded for changes in the probability of exposure to threats and to violence itself. In this way quite fine gradations could in principle be valued. Police output could be expressed in terms of these probabilities, and in this way commensurability of input with output achieved.

What offenders gain from murder, rape and so on is also difficult to value. If offenders are aware of the probability of apprehension and of the punishment they are likely to receive, then the expected value of the loss from punishment might serve as a guide, though what relationship this would bear to readily measured variables such as income is not certain.

It is therefore no easier to value crimes of violence than theft. However, if we can be sure that crimes of violence involve more 'bads' per incidence than the corresponding traffic accidents, then valuations of the latter can be used as minima in the same way as the amount stolen can be taken as a minimum measure of the social loss from theft. Whether the methods used to value traffic accidents are themselves conceptually well-based is an issue that will not be pursued here. For example, loss of earnings have been mentioned above, but earnings themselves do not constitute an index of welfare.

TRAFFIC OFFENCES

The aim of special regulations governing traffic is to reduce accidents or to save motorists time or money. (The aim of recent reductions in speed limits in the United Kingdom is principally to induce motorists to act as if the shadow price of fuel were the actual price.) The benefits of these regulations are already valued for road-investment purposes and these values are of course appropriate in the present context. On the offenders' side (of course offenders are also potential victims, but leave that aside) the penalty unique to driving offences (why?), suspension of the licence to drive, might be valued as the loss of consumers' surplus that would have been derived from the use of a car during the period of suspension, and this would not be easy to measure. But would it be impossible? In order to appraise road investments, it is customary to build models of trip generation and distribution, often of a 'gravity' type, where the number of trips made to a set of destinations can be described as

$$T_j = kA_j f(C_j),$$

where T_j is the number of trips from a particular origin to destination j, k is a constant, A_j is the attractiveness of j relative to other destinations, and C_j is the cost in terms of both time and money of reaching *j*. This relationship could in principle be expressed as a demand for *j* (see Figure 5). If C_j^0 is the actual cost of reaching destination *j* from the origin in question, then the banning of all motorists would result in a loss of consumers' surplus represented by the shaded area. No doubt this amount could be adjusted to represent the loss to only one motorist, for example by the simple expedient of dividing by the number of

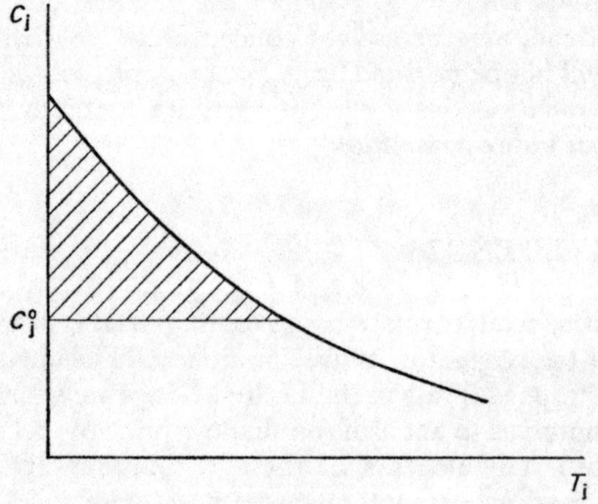

FIG. 5

motorists to which the curve refers. Any gravity model worth its salt will be able to generate the demand curves for all other destinations as a result of a rise in the price (cost) of destination *j* from C_j^0 to infinity, or at least to a level at which trips to *j* are choked off. The next thing to do is to value the loss of destination *k* on the assumption that *j* is not available (and this would be greater than if *k* were to be lost but not *j*, provided *k* and *j* are to some extent substitutes), and so on until there are no destinations left. This sequential method for calculating surplus is that recommended by Mishan ([11], ch. 8), extending the argument of Hicks ([12], ch. XVIII).

However, this analysis effectively values a punishment and so properly belongs to the next chapter. Only a slight change in

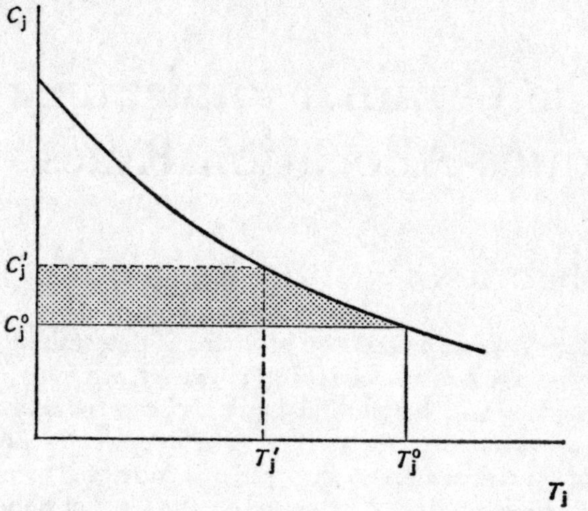

FIG. 6

method is needed to reveal consumers' valuations of changes in the regulations or the zeal with which these are enforced. For example, the change could be the introduction of the breathalyser, or a lowering of speed limits. Any reduction of the number of trips to a destination could be valued using a gravity model. Suppose that, before the change, a cost of $C_j{}^0$ was generating $T_j{}^0$ trips to destination j. Afterwards, it may be found that only $T_j{}'$ trips are made to j. We know from the curve $T_j = kA_jf(C_j)$, the value of C_j that would produce this number of trips (call it $C_j{}'$). The loss of surplus from the change is therefore given by the dotted area, and that, suitably aggregated over all destinations with due attention being paid to the difficulties in calculating changes in surplus in a context of substitute destinations with 'prices' changing simultaneously, is consumers' subjective valuation of the change.

5 The Optimal Punishment: Police-Allocation Rules

INTRODUCTION

In Chapter 2 we discussed the problem of determining p and f when both were control variables. However, we must recognise that an agency which can adjust one of the variables may have no control over the other. The police typically have little influence on the sentences imposed on convicted persons and the courts have no direct influence on the level of police inputs or their disposition. It is therefore worthwhile exploring rules for sub-optimisation. We consider both variables in turn.

THE OPTIMAL PUNISHMENT

What should be the value of f per offence? Casting back to the exposition of Becker's analysis in Chapter 2 we see that, in equilibrium ($\partial L/\partial f=0$),

$$e_{\mathrm{f}}=\frac{bpf}{D'+C'+bpf}.$$

Recall that D' is marginal damage per offence and C' is marginal cost of apprehension per offence. For present purposes this expression can usefully be restated:

$$f=\frac{D'+C'}{\left(\dfrac{1}{e_{\mathrm{f}}}-1\right)bp}.$$

It has already been established that for the optimal level of offences, $e_{\mathrm{f}}<1$. The expression $\left(\dfrac{1}{e_{\mathrm{f}}}-1\right)$, then, is positive.

Hence f varies inversely with p, the probability of apprehension, and with b, the social cost of punishment. f varies directly with D', that is the more the net damage caused by an offence the higher the optimal punishment, a result which clearly conforms with current practice and with common sense. f also varies with C', the marginal cost of apprehension. The last two effects can be summed up as follows: the greater the marginal net damage from an offence and the more costly to apprehend the miscreant, the more it will pay to sustain social loss through punishment in order to deter the offence. f is directly related to e_f – the higher the elasticity of the offence with respect to the punishment, the higher the optimal level of punishment; the corollary is that if the level of offences is unresponsive to punishment, there is no point in punishing if cost is involved. Remember that Becker's model relates only to the criminal prospect and that the only effect of punishment is therefore deterrence. However, where punishment is custodial, it is possible to reduce the level of offences even among offenders who do not respond to expected penalties – by denying them the opportunity to commit further crimes. Furthermore, punishment is not the only aim of treatment of convicts. In cases where offenders are mentally disturbed, for example (notably) baby-snatchers and shoplifters, often only token punishment is imposed if the convict undertakes to accept treatment the aim of which is to reduce future propensity to offend. Note too that e_f does not relate solely to the potential offender who actually is convicted and punished – it refers to the effect of punishment on all potential offenders. It may therefore pay to punish someone wholly unresponsive if others are likely to alter their behaviour in response to that individual's fate. The execution of the unfortunate Admiral Byng *pour encourager les autres* is a celebrated example.

The view is often heard that it is pointless to jail offenders if their post-release behaviour is not changed. As we have seen, there are at least two reasons why it might not be pointless: (*a*) the preventive effect of detention and (*b*) the effect on others. This view is but a special instance of the proposition that treatment is better than punishment. It may of course be true that, at present, the mix of treatment and punishment is excessively heavy in the punitive element, but the use of the word 'excessively' is only meaningful if we have some notion of an optimal mix. Even if there were a switch from punishment, which we will assume to have no impact on convicts' subsequent careers, to treatment, which (let us suppose) is wholly successful in extirpating recidivism, the switch might not be efficient if, for example, the reduction in social cost in processing the convict is outweighed by an increase in the social cost of offences committed by others – presuming that the social cost of treatment is lower but that its deterrent effect is lower too. In effect for treatment f would be low (if it were zero offenders might turn themselves in, and indeed they sometimes do even in present circumstances) but b would be high because care inputs would be required.

MORE THAN ONE FORM OF PUNISHMENT

Hitherto we have discussed optimal punishment in a setting where there was only one form of punishment. Now we analyse the choice between two forms: imprisonment and fine. Let us denote units of imprisonment by j, units of fine by m. What is the rule for choosing between fines and jail for an offence? If the two forms of punishment are alternatives, the rule is to choose that for which L, total social loss, is lower for the optimum level of offences in each case. Fines, then, are to be preferred to jail as $L^m < L^j$. Let $\bar{O}^m$, $\bar{O}^j$ be the optimum level of offences in each case. Fines are preferable if

$$D(\bar{O}^m) + C(\bar{O}^m, p) + b_m pm\bar{O}^m < D(\bar{O}^j) + C(\bar{O}^j, p) + b_j pj\bar{O}^j.$$

The *prima facie* case for fines is this. If other things are equal, $b_m \to 0$ since fines are transfers from one set of people to another. Now $b_j > 0$. Therefore fines are preferable to jail sentences. However, for serious offences (D' is high) the optimal level of m may be so high that it cannot be collected. Then $b_m \to \infty$, or more generally, $b_m > b_j$ and a jail sentence becomes the appropriate punishment for such crimes.

But even for lesser crimes the superiority of fines cannot be guaranteed because of the possibility that $\bar{O}^j \neq \bar{O}^m$. In order to develop the correct rule for fines versus jail for a type of offence it is helpful to rearrange the expression for $\partial L/\partial f=0$. We have already used two arrangements at the beginning of this chapter. Now we use a third, that is

$$D'+C'=-bpf\left(1-\frac{1}{e_f}\right).$$

This is the formulation Becker himself uses. He interprets the left-hand side as the marginal cost of permitting a rise in the level of offences through a reduction in f and the right-hand side as the marginal benefit from so doing. Note that for an optimum $(\partial L/\partial f=0)$ the right-hand side must be positive, a necessary condition for which being that $e_f<1$ since $b, p, f>0$.

Now consider the two alternative forms of punishment:

$$D'+C'=-b_m pm\left(1-\frac{1}{e_m}\right)$$

and

$$D'+C'=-b_j pj\left(1-\frac{1}{e_j}\right).$$

Notice that the left-hand side is the same for both. The marginal cost of offences, no matter what the form of punishment used, is the same. The marginal-cost and marginal-benefit schedules can be shown against the number of offences.

In Figure 7 we see that at $\bar{O}_j$, $MB_j=MC$, but $MB_m<MC$,

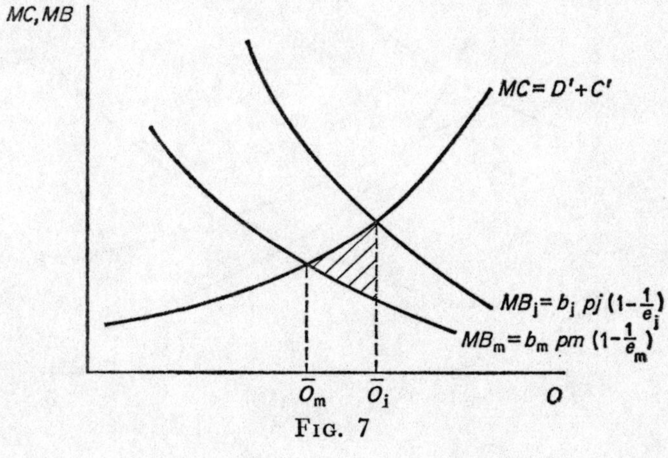

FIG. 7

that is the marginal cost of permitting an increase in O is greater than the marginal benefit. A switch to fines, set to induce $\bar{O}^m$ offences, produces a net benefit represented by the shaded area.

We assumed above that $b_m < b_j$. However this is not a sufficient condition for preferring fines. For the elasticity of offences with respect to fines might be less than that with respect to jail sentences, or $e_m < e_j$. Thus the MB_m schedule might lie above the MB_j schedule, even if $b_m < b_j$ and jail would therefore be better than fines.

What if neither schedule lies wholly above the other? The only point of significance to note is that a change in the level of the MC schedule, for example a rise from MC_1 to MC_2, would mean a switch from fining to jailing (see Figure 8). Such a rise might be caused by an increase in D' for example. A cross-over in the MB schedules might be due to a fall of e_m relative to e_j when a lower level of offences is to be induced, i.e. much crime is to be prevented. Of course it is possible for the MB schedules to coincide over a range of levels of offences. Then there would be an option. But it is reasonable to suppose that jail cannot be small enough for some offences – for example dropping litter –

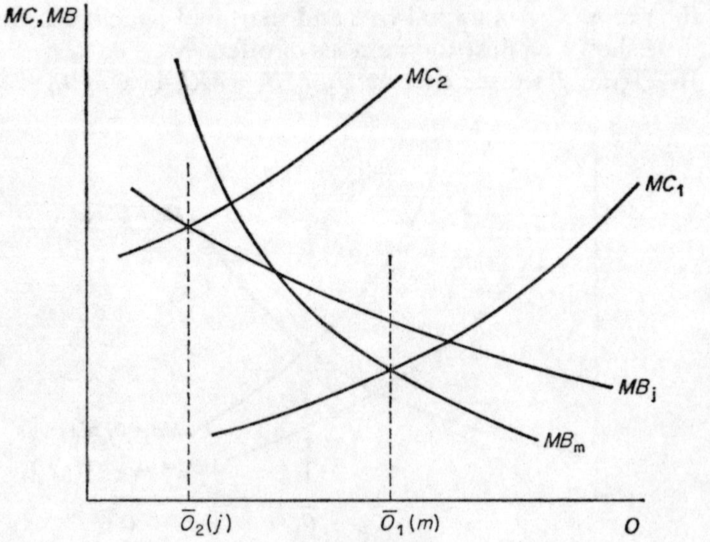

Fig. 8

and fines cannot be large enough for others – such as homicide.

For present purposes an offence may be defined in the normal way, by reference to the act committed, but equally it may be convenient to define according to the characteristics of the offender. The relative rankings of e_j and e_m might differ between categories of offender for the same offence: it may be sensible to fine a first offender and jail a recidivist.

There is perhaps one last point worth mentioning. From Figure 9 there may seem to be a conflict between the marginal and total conditions for an optimum, in that at $\bar{O}_j$ fines are to be preferred with an optimum level of offences at $\bar{O}_m$. Yet inspection of the diagram reveals that total loss using jail is

$$\sum_{O=0}^{\bar{O}_j} (MB_j + MC)$$

and that is less than the corresponding measure using fines,

$$\sum_{O=0}^{\bar{O}_m} (MB_m + MC).$$

The problem is resolved as follows. The marginal benefit schedule represents what is gained by allowing an increase in the number of offences. At O_1, j would have been chosen, so that what is saved by allowing an increase in offences beyond O_1 is the cost of jail, not the higher cost of fines. Thus the appropriate MB curve for measuring L is the envelope of MB curves consisting of the MB curve of the form of punishment whose MB is lowest for any particular level of offences – $ABCD$ in Figure 9. Notice that the maximand is not the area between the MB and MC curves, which is what it would be in the case of a normal good where the MB curve is a marginal-valuation curve. In fact the area between the curves is a minimand not a maximand. The reason is that in this case loss $L = TC + TB$ (because of the nature of the benefit), whereas with a normal good $L = TC - TB$ (where $TB = \sum MV$).

POLICE-ALLOCATION RULES

Whatever the optimum punishment, the level, mix and deployment of police inputs must be determined in a context in which

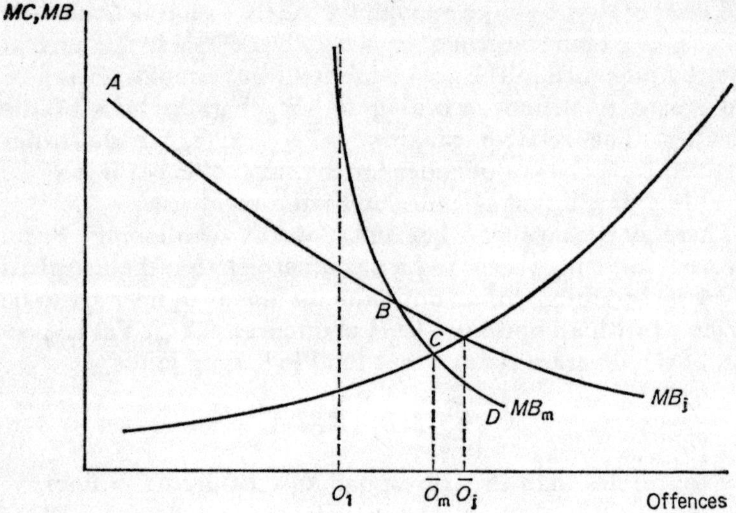

FIG. 9

the amount of punishment is not a control variable: the police typically have little control over the sentence imposed, sentencing being a function of the judiciary, an independent agency. Yet the benefits of police action – which we will identify as offences prevented – are jointly produced by the criminal justice system as a whole. If the 'correction agencies' were wholly ineffective in altering the subsequent careers of offenders and in addition had no deterrent effect there would be little point in the police detecting and apprehending offenders, save perhaps for the possibility that if custodial sentences were imposed offenders might commit fewer crimes through being out of circulation for a while. And the costs of securing the benefits are the costs of the separate agencies of the system added together. An interesting corollary is that if the productivity of the agencies downstream of the police changes, the optimal level of police input will change too.

The rule for the police administration is therefore to select the level of operations so as to equate the marginal social costs *to the whole C.J.S.* with the marginal social value of prevented offences. Note that it is therefore incorrect for the police to equate marginal costs to their own budget with the marginal social value of prevented offences, although it would of course seem at first sight to be the natural thing to do.

With this in mind, it is necessary to say a little more about costs. Clearly, police administrations need more cost information than most organisations. As an illustration, suppose the police can prevent crime in two ways: (*a*) by maintaining a conspicuous presence in the more crime-prone areas, and (*b*) by detection and apprehension of offenders – the problem being how much of each to do. The costs of preventive patrol are simply police costs. The effectiveness of preventive patrol does of course depend on offenders' disinclination to exposure to correction agencies, but changes in preventions due to changes in the intensity of preventive patrol do not impose additional costs on agencies of the C.J.S. downstream of the police; actual detection and apprehension do give rise to downstream costs. Therefore, in determining the mix of (*a*) and (*b*), the administration does need downstream cost information. In the appendix to this chapter we show how to derive these rules from Becker's L function. One way of providing the necessary cost information in a comprehensive way is to simulate the actual behaviour of system. A noteworthy example of this approach is to be found in Blumstein and Larson [13]. First of all each processing stage in the system is identified. The input to each stage is described by a vector whose ith element represents the yearly flow attributable to characteristic i, which would normally be a type of offence but might be any other relevant feature of the flow. Each processing stage is characterised by a vector of cost rates, calculated as average costs to the public purse, but there is no reason why marginal social costs should not be used. The flow of output from that stage is distributed to the elements of the next stage by reference to a vector of branching probabilities. Clearly where there are potential differences in the inflow and outflow of a stage per unit period (as with prisons for example), a more complex cost function with capacity constraints is needed. In this way it would be possible to trace the downstream costs of an increase in detections, or, more generally, any change in police practice – in short to generate the information necessary to operate the allocation rule.

To match this cost information it is necessary to generate similar information as to benefit. This involves the need to elucidate C.J.S. production functions. The consultants Arthur Andersen [14] have made some estimates of the number and type of future offences prevented as a result of an offender's detection and process through the C.J.S. as compared with his non-detection. Various studies emanating from the Operations Research Department at Lancaster University (see, for example [15]) have sought to establish the production function for police resources in terms of (*a*) preventions and (*b*) detections. Combination of the results of these two pieces of work would yield a production function for police resources in terms of prevented crimes. Notice that this approach to establishing a production function is an alternative to Ehrlich's approach of cross-sectional statistical analysis which was discussed in Chapter 3.

APPENDIX

A loss function slightly different from Becker's is used in that it is assumed that $C(p, O) = C(pO)$. Let $A = pO$. A is the number of arrests, which for simplicity are assumed equal to the number of convictions, that is

$$L = D(O) + C(A) + bfA.$$

Instead of minimising L with respect to p, A is chosen as the control variable:

$$\frac{\partial L}{\partial A} = \frac{\partial D(O)}{\partial A} + C_A + bf = 0.$$

It is plausible to suppose that $\partial D(O)/\partial A < 0$: a rise in the arrest rate will reduce the number of offences and hence D, net damage from offences. $C_A > 0$, that is the marginal cost of arrests is positive. $bf > 0$ since both the social and subjective private costs of punishment are positive. Rearranging terms,

$$-\frac{\partial D}{\partial A} = C_A + bf.$$

The left-hand side represents the marginal value of prevented offences, and the right-hand side the marginal cost of preventing them via arrests. The important point to note is that the latter includes costs incurred downstream of the police. $\partial D/\partial A$ is a measure of the effectiveness of the correction agencies. If $\partial D/\partial A = 0$, then for equilibrium $C_A = 0$ is necessary. This can only be so if no resources are devoted to making arrests.

The rule for allocating police resources between prevention and detection can be found by adding the cost of units of preventive patrol, B, to the loss function:

$$L = D(O) + C(A) + C(B) + bfA.$$

Differentiating partially with respect to A and B and setting the results at zero,

$$\frac{\partial L}{\partial A} = \frac{\partial D}{\partial A} + C_A + bf$$

and

$$\frac{\partial L}{\partial B} = \frac{\partial D}{\partial B} + C_B.$$

From which,

$$-\frac{\partial D}{\partial A} + \frac{\partial D}{\partial B} = C_A + bf - C_B.$$

The difference in benefit from devoting resources to preventive patrol rather than making arrests must be equated with the difference in costs from doing so, where the costs of arrests are again defined to include downstream costs, bf.

6 Downstream Costs of Crime Prevention

In the previous chapter we saw that the net social value of a particular number of arrests is the value of offences prevented less the the police costs and downstream costs (bf) required to prevent them. It is now time to turn our attention to enumeration and valuation of the elements composing b and to value f.

Let us dispose of court costs first of all. These comprise the market prices of resources needed to handle the relevant increment in throughput, provided that all social costs are counted, including the opportunity costs of jurors' and witnesses' time and the costs of providing legal representation for defendants, and not merely calls on the public purse.

The treatment of the costs of buildings and staff used by the prison service could no doubt be assimilated to that of the courts. The main problems arise in assessing the prisoner-related costs of custody. The change-in-net-output method might be used. Loss is measured by

+value of prisoners' output outside prison
−value of prisoners' outside consumption
−value of prisoners' output inside prison
+value of prisoners' inside consumption.

This is a measure of what *other* members of the community lose through custody of convicts. The problem of what to do about what the income-tax prisoners might have contributed to the rest of society is implicitly solved by taking the difference between output and consumption. The higher the income tax the higher will this gap be. Of course it follows that the higher the level of income tax the more society loses through imprisonment of offenders. Another interesting implication is that the better off the offender is the higher is the cost to society from imprisoning him because he pays more income tax.

Any net saving prisoners had been undertaking outside would have to be subtracted from the above on the grounds that to save is simply to postpone consumption and not to forgo it, and the benefit to the rest of society is exactly offset (at the margin) by interest payments. Similarly, any net dissaving would have to be added.

There is another complication. Provided that the value of outside consumption is measured at market price at the point of sale – probably the easiest way to measure it – there is the problem of how to treat commodity taxation and subsidy. The answer is to subtract subsidies from the measure of loss from imprisonment – the rest of society no longer loses these – and add in taxes – the rest of society no longer gains these. The problem of the consumption of commodities rationed in whole or part other than by price resembles that of subsidy. For example, suppose that a prisoner had been occupying rent-controlled accommodation. Its net value to the rest of society is what would be paid for the usufruct right, that is 'key money'.

One or two corollaries emerge from this analysis. Notice that the social loss of imprisoning those who were unemployed might be negative. If prisoners fare no better from the point of view of consumption than the unemployed, inside and outside consumption cancel out. Since outside output is of course zero, inside production is a net gain to society. Secondly, the more an individual eschews heavily taxed wines and spirits and the more he subsists on government-subsidised basic foodstuffs the less society loses by imprisoning him.

But what if prisoners' gains and losses are to be counted too? How would these be measured? There are certain affinities between loss of life and loss of freedom. A satisfactory measure might be the value of life used in transport planning, suitably adjusted to allow for the fact that terms of imprisonment are finite. The loss consists in being denied the opportunity freely to take decisions about production and consumption; it is not clear how well a measure based on the value of life captures this. However, we can circumvent this problem by arguing that a zero value should be placed on offenders' loss of liberty since they voluntarily assume the risks of capture and imprisonment, and the subjective value of these 'bads' is already reflected in the rewards they derive from offending. To place a positive value on loss of liberty at this stage would therefore involve double-counting. We are therefore spared a great difficulty. Of course, the subjective value of f can be found by manipulating the expression first seen in Chapter 4,

$$f = \frac{(w_i - w_1)(\lambda - p\lambda + p)}{p}.$$

To value f we would need to know what the probability of capture is, and, even more difficult, what forgone legitimate earnings are, and, even more difficult still, λ, the ratio of the marginal utility of wealth in the uncaught state to that in the caught state. It therefore seems better to deal with the problem in the process of assessing the rewards from offending. It will be recalled that at the margin the amount stolen, w_i, captures all the costs of offending.

An important, and perhaps rather surprising, result of this analysis is that whether offenders' gains and losses are to count or not, we do not need a direct measure of offenders' losses from imprisonment.

This is a convenient point at which to pause to summarise the social net gains to be derived from reductions in the number of offences via changes in C.J.S. control variables, making various assumptions about the social weight to be attached to offenders' gains and losses. Let us take the particular example of increasing the number of arrests. The basic equation (it will be recalled from the appendix to the previous chapter) is

$$-\frac{\partial D}{\partial A} = C_A + bf.$$

What is the gain from preventing offences? If all gains and losses are to count then the transfer, w_i, cancels out. Offenders' opportunity costs, $w_1 + [pf/(p + \lambda - p\lambda)]$, equal to w_i at the margin, are saved. Victims may save the cost of some preventive measures, k. Each arrest may prevent more than or less than one offence. The cost of an extra arrest is the incremental police cost, C_A. The social cost of punishment, bf, does not include the offender's subjective costs, but only costs to the rest of society, the change in net output and prison buildings and staff. This means that we have to interpret f as a physical measure and b as a monetary measure (£s per unit of f), whereas hitherto we have been interpreting f as offenders' subjective valuation of punishment and b as unity (in order to give full weight to offenders' valuation) plus the cost to the rest of society per £'s worth of offenders' valuation.

Now suppose that offenders' gains and losses are not to count at all. Then the gain from preventing a theft is the amount that ceases to be transferred – w_i – plus k. The cost of arrest and punishment is treated as above. In fact, if punishment is by imprisonment the net social gains from arrests are the same whether offenders' losses and gains are to count or not.

Now suppose that offenders' losses are to count but not gains. Then the net gain from offence-prevention is greater than on either of the two previous assumptions by offenders' opportunity costs, $w_1 + [pf/(p+\lambda-p\lambda)]$, and this is approximated by w_i.

If punishment is by fine, the only change is that f is a money measure, the amount of the fine and b is equal to -1 plus enforcement costs expressed as £s per £ of fine.

7 Concluding Remarks

PUNISHMENT

It should perhaps be emphasised that in the schema employed in this book there is no place for any retributive element in punishment. Indeed, retribution is strictly incompatible with the conception of punishment used here. For punishment here is conceived of as an efficient, in varying degrees non-transferable, stochastic price. Efficiency is defined in the normal way in which in welfare-economic analysis prices are adjudged efficient or not, taking into account the features of partial non-transferability and stochasticness. Punishment prices are stochastic in that they are charged not with certainty, only with a degree of probability. A price is said to be non-transferable if to the loser who pays there corresponds no gainer who receives payment. Even fines may be partly non-transferable on account of collection costs.

If a retributive element is added to an efficient punishment price, it ceases to be efficient. Only if the retributive element of a sentence is to run concurrently with the efficient-price element can the two approaches be said to be compatible and in such a case of course there is in effect no retributive element at all, in which case if society wishes to express outrage at a criminal's deeds a statement from the judge would seem to offer the only way of doing so.

CONSUMPTION OF DRUGS

The problem of what is popularly termed 'drug abuse' is one of inelasticity of demand within a short period, even when price is very high, coupled with a very high, indeed infinite, rate of time preference. When the cost of financing a given level of consumption begins to exceed what the consumer can earn by legitimate means, it is plainly in his interests to consider any illicit opportunity to supplement his income. (In terms of the kind of analysis presented in Chapter 1, $f_i = 0$ because of high time preference. We therefore have the case of $w_i - w_l > f_i$. This is a sufficient condition for specialisation in illegitimate activity so long as $w_i > w_l$ over the whole range of t, the time devoted to non-leisure. It may be, however, that $(dw_i/dt_i) < 0$, with the possibility that, before t is exhausted, $w_l > w_i$. In such a case it would be worth the drug consumer's while to divide his time between working and offending.) The trouble is that illicit opportunity in this case tends to mean violent robbery. It is not clear whether the practice of drug consumption in itself induces a disinclination for regular work and a disposition to ruthless violence. In any case the point is of little *analytical* importance. If the objective of anti-drug activities is to reduce the amount of crime, then the policy of controlling the supply, and therefore raising the price, may have been counter-productive on account of the inelasticity of demand. However, the policy of controlling supply has itself been ineffective and was doomed to be so (Holahan [16]), though of course prices have been kept high.

Given that prices have been kept high, what are the implications for a Becker-type model of crime control? Due to the high time-preference element, the deterrent effect of punishment will be low. There is no form of treatment which has much effect on offenders' subsequent drug consumption (Blair and Vogel [17]), and it can surely be presumed that the former level of offending is likewise resumed. The only point of punishing offenders is therefore preventive detention. In Chapter 5, the following formula for the optimum punishment was derived:

$$f = \frac{D' + C'}{\left(\frac{1}{e_f} - 1\right) bp}.$$

The analysis of Chapter 5 would probably show a fine to be inappropriate. We therefore concentrate on imprisonment. Contrary to the usual assumption in the drug-related-offences case that $e_f \to 0$ (and therefore $f \to 0$), a proposition that is true when deterrent and rehabilitative effects only are considered (again, see Blair and Vogel [17]), we may assume that e_f is well-behaved since drug consumers can be expected to commit fewer crimes inside an institution of preventive detention than outside. C' may be high because offenders may make strenuous efforts to elude capture once it becomes imminent and they may be difficult to identify. For the same reasons p may be low. In these circumstances f may be high. This will normally mean that social cost, though minimised with respect to f, will be high too. However, it is possible that C' and p could both be changed dramatically if offenders were offered their normal dose in captivity; they might even turn themselves in. In these circumstances custodial costs might also be greatly reduced. However, the nature of the punishment must be carefully modulated so as to prevent its becoming attractive to those who would not otherwise commit crimes, the danger being that social cost might again be higher than necessary. No doubt this desideratum would be satisfied so long as the custodial problem were one of keeping people in rather than keeping them out.

What, however, of drug consumers who do not commit crimes? The problem is then said to be that 'a large segment of society could become unproductive and become parasites on that segment of society that is less self-indulgent' (Blair and Vogel [17]) – in other words drug consumers leave the labour force. Culyer ([18], p. 455) admirably disposes of the argument that the loss of output constitutes a social disbenefit: 'As far as the loss of GDP is concerned, this should concern us, for marginal withdrawals from the labour force, only insofar as wages do not reflect the social value of an individual's product.' In other words, while the rest of society loses the output of someone who opts out, his claim on the rest of society's output is no longer met since he ceases to be paid. What, then, of Blair and Vogel's 'parasites'? One answer that might be given is that those who leave the labour force are normally granted a state subvention to the extent of which they can continue to exercise a claim on the rest of society's output. The rest of society therefore loses, to the extent of the subvention, when someone opts out. But in evaluating the net social disbenefit of opting out it is necessary to remember that 'opters out' are themselves also members of society. The subvention is but a transfer. Opters out gain £x. The remainder of society loses £x. Moreover, if someone opts out then he is, in his own estimation, surely better off, otherwise he would not have done so. Is there not therefore some net gain? No. At best there is no net loss. Let us suppose that the decision to leave the labour force is an all-or-nothing one, that is a worker can accept or decline employment in 40-hour-week units at an hourly wage of $\bar{w}$. *BS* is the individual's supply curve.

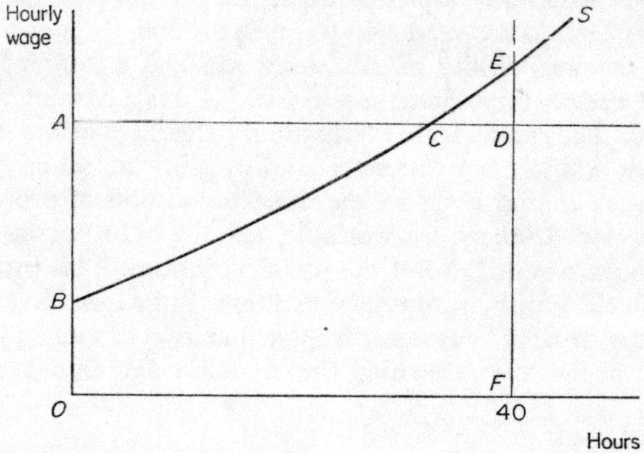

FIG. 10

His surplus is $ABC-ECD(>0)$. He will decline employment if the state subvention (also, let us suppose, all or nothing) is such that $S>ABC-ECD$. At most $S=ABC-ECD$ for an opter out. The opter out loses $ABC-ECD$ and gains S. The rest of society loses S. S cancels out for society as a whole. The net social cost arising from someone opting out is therefore, at most, $ABC-ECD$, the surplus from work. Even, then, if there were no consumers' surplus on the output valued at *AOFD* (Culyer's point), it is wrong to conclude that there is therefore no social loss. This argument clearly applies also to those who opt out for reasons unrelated to drug consumption. The point of the immediately preceding argument is that the consumption of drugs may involve society in social loss even where no offences are committed. It appears that there is a case for social policy so concern itself with 'drug abuse', though what form concern thould take it is not easy to say, particularly in view of what is said in the next-but-one paragraph.

Notice that we have not been considering the question whether drug consumption should be legalised or not; we have been concerned with the welfare-theoretic optimal treatment of criminals who are drug users and with the question whether society sustains social loss through drug-related departures from the labour force. It is hoped that clarification of these questions will be of help to the reader in forming his own judgements.

Does the availability of subsidised medical treatment constitute a reason for official suppression of drug consumption? The *prima facie* reason is that individuals who have access to free treatment consume treatment to the point at which their marginal valuation is below marginal social cost of provision. Smokers and drinkers, for example, are likely to pursue their habits to an extent beyond the social optimum. This problem can be dealt with by sumptuary taxation. But as we have seen, rises in the price of drugs may induce increases in violent crime without necessarily affecting the demand for free medical services.

TAX EVASION AND SHOPLIFTING

There are certain advantages in considering these together. Tax evasion essentially consists in shoplifting publicly provided goods. Allingham and Sandmo [19] analyse the taxpayer's private optimum rate of evasion. Kolm [20] identifies the problem of enforcement as one in which the authorities' maximand is the aggregate of representative citizens' utilities of private and public goods less enforcement costs, on the assumption that taxpayers act so as to maximise their expected utility, the level of any individual's consumption of public goods being independent of his tax contribution. An interesting corollary to emerge when the authorities' decision variable is the tax rate is that the marginal private value of public funds is given by

$$\frac{1}{1-\left(1-\frac{p\pi}{\theta}\right) E_\theta{}^{X}},$$

where p is the probability of discovery of evasion, π is the punitive tax rate levied on unsuccessfully concealed taxable £s and $E_\theta{}^{X}$ is the elasticity of reported income with respect to the tax rate. Allingham and Sandmo show that $\theta > p\pi$ for an internal solution (some but not all income is declared). If $E_\theta{}^{X}$ can be presumed negative (taxpayers response to rising tax rates by reducing the amount of income they declare), this expression is greater than unity.

What is the practical importance of this result? To take but one example, it means that when a public project is to be financed by taxation it is important to recognise that the opportunity cost of the funds exceeds their face value, so that a shadow price has to be applied. As yet, no actual figure has been derived for this purpose.

For the firm, shoplifting is rather like sales taxation. We will not attempt a comprehensive discussion of this topic, but it will be of interest to consider the view that is occasionally heard that shoplifting has desirable redistributive effects in that shoplifters are poor and shop-owners are rich. An elementary appreciation of the theory of tax-shifting shows that the incidence of the 'tax' burden casts doubt on the fact of redistribution from rich to poor. Suppose that shoplifting is differentially great in certain geographical areas, for example ghettoes of the poor. The supply of capital for use in such areas will be elastic at the generally prevailing rate of return. If there is any degree of elasticity of demand below infinity for locally merchandised goods in the ghetto, prices will settle at a higher level there to yield shop-owners the going rate of return on capital. In that case the 'tax' burden is shifted to consumers in the ghetto and the redistribution is from the poor in general to the dishonest poor. If there is very elastic demand in the ghetto above prices prevailing elsewhere, shops will not be established there but *ex hypothesi* the loss of convenience will be small. If shoplifting is not confined to particular areas there may be shifting to consumers in general if the elasticity of supply of capital to retailing is high, and the transfer will be from the honest to the dishonest.

However, for shop-owners, shoplifting may be unlike a sales tax in being easier to 'evade'. An increase in surveillance and a reduction in the openness of display of goods may reduce shoplifting depredations, a case analysed for a comprehensive welfare function by Skogh [21]. Indeed if these measures are generally employed, it will be impossible to achieve the going rate of return without them.

References and Bibliography

[1] I. Ehrlich, 'Participation in Illegitimate Activities: A Theoretical and Empirical Investigation', *Journal of Political Economy* (1973).

[2] G. S. Becker, 'Crime and Punishment: An Economic Approach', *Journal of Political Economy* (1968).

[3] H. A. J. Green, *Consumer Theory* (Harmondsworth: Penguin, 1971).

[4] G. J. Stigler, 'Optimum Enforcement of Laws', *Journal of Political Economy* (1970).

[5] J. I. Chapman, W. Z. Hirsch and S. Sonenblum, 'A Police Service Production Function' (unpublished manuscript).

[6] R. A. Carr-Hill and N. H. Stern, 'An Econometric Model of the Supply and Control of Recorded Offences in England and Wales', *Journal of Public Economics* (1973).

[7] G. Tullock, 'The Welfare Costs of Tariffs, Monopolies, and Theft', *Western Economic Journal* (1967).

[8] D. C. Shoup and S. L. Mehay, *Program Budgeting for Urban Police Services* (U.C.L.A.: Institute of Government and Public Affairs, 1971).

[9] I. Ehrlich and G. S. Becker, 'Market Insurance, Self-Insurance and Self-Protection', *Journal of Political Economy* (1972).

[10] R. L. Carter, *Theft in the Market* (London: Institute for Economic Affairs, 1974).

[11] E. J. Mishan, *Cost–Benefit Analysis* (London: Allen & Unwin, 1971).

[12] J. R. Hicks, *A Revision of Demand Theory* (Oxford University Press, 1956).

[13] A. Blumstein and R. Larson, 'Models of a Total Criminal Justice System', *Operations Research* (1969).

[14] A. Andersen & Co., *Some Numerical Estimates of the Effectiveness of the Criminal Justice System* (unpublished, 1968).

[15] J. W. Bryant, M. L. Chambers and D. Falcon, *Patrol Effectiveness and Patrol Deployment* (unpublished, 1968).

[16] J. Holahan, 'The Economics of Control of the Illegal Supply of Heroin', *Public Finance Quarterly* (1973).

[17] R. D. Blair and R. J. Vogel, 'Heroin Addiction and Urban Crime', *Public Finance Quarterly* (1973).
[18] A. J. Culyer, 'Should Social Policy Concern Itself with Drug "Abuse"?', *Public Finance Quarterly* (1973).
[19] M. G. Allingham and A. Sandmo, 'Income Tax Evasion: A Theoretical Analysis', *Journal of Public Economics* (1972).
[20] S.-Ch. Kolm, 'A Note on Optimum Tax Evasion', *Journal of Public Economics* (1973).
[21] G. Skogh, 'En samhällsekonomisk mål-medel-analys av butiksnatterier', in Swedish Government Official Report, SOU 1971:10, *Snatteri* (1971).
[22] S. Rottenberg, 'The Clandestine Distribution of Heroin, Its Discovery and Suppression', *Journal of Political Economy* (1968).
[23] R. A. Fernandez, 'The Clandestine Distribution of Heroin, Its Discovery and Suppression: A Comment', *Journal of Political Economy* (1968).
[24] E. Erickson, 'The Social Costs of the Discovery and Suppression of the Clandestine Distribution of Heroin', *Journal of Political Economy* (1968).
[25] K. L. Avio, 'An Economic Analysis of Criminal Corrections: The Canadian Case', *Canadian Journal of Economics* (1973).
[26] C. S. Shoup, 'Standards for Distributing a Free Governmental Service: Crime Prevention', *Public Finance* (1964).
[27] D. Dosser, 'Notes on Carl S. Shoup's "Standards for Distributing a Free Governmental Service: Crime Prevention" ', *Public Finance* (1964).
[28] W. M. Landes, 'An Economic Analysis of the Courts', *Journal of Law and Economics* (1971).
[29] J. Baldry, 'Positive Economic Analysis of Criminal Behaviour', in *Economic Policies and Social Goals*, ed. A. J. Culyer (London: Martin Robertson, 1974).
[30] G. Skogh, 'A Note on Gary Becker's "Crime and Punishment: An Economic Approach" ', *Swedish Journal of Economics* (1973).
[31] G. Skogh, *Straffratt och samhällsekonomi* (Lund, Sweden: Lund Economic Studies, 1973). In Swedish, with a very good summary in English. Considers the welfare-theoretic basis for the law as well as for law enforcement. Points out that in the case of shoplifting a marginal substitution of private for public preventive measures might yield a net social benefit, this to be obtained by decriminalising small first-time offences: the police take names but do not prosecute.

[32] H. Tulkens and A. Jacquemin, *The Cost of Delinquency: A Problem of Optimal Allocation of Private and Public Expenditures* (CORE Discussion Paper, Catholic University of Louvain, Belgium, 1971). They make the assumption that public preventive measures are public goods in the Samuelson sense, while private preventive measures are private goods.

[33] D. L. Martin, 'The Economics of Jury Conscription', *Journal of Political Economy* (1972).

[34] A. D. Neu, 'Penal Sentencing in Germany: Some Economic Aspects', *Public Finance* (1972).